To:

....

From:

....

Date:

....

THE WONDER OF CREATION

100 MORE DEVOTIONS
ABOUT GOD & SCIENCE

LOUIE GIGLIO
WITH TAMA FORTNER

ILLUSTRATED BY NICOLA ANDERSON

passionpublishing

Tommy NELSON

An Imprint of Thomas Nelson

CONTENTS

INTRODUCTION

Hello, explorer!

My name is Pastor Louie. I've been fascinated by science and space since I was your age, and I am amazed by God and *all* of His creation! Whether you've already read my other two books about science and faith, *Indescribable* and *How Great Is Our God,* or you're new to the Indescribable Kids family, welcome! I can't wait to jump into this new adventure and explore the wonder of creation together!

I'm a curious person, and I bet you are too. For example, have you ever wondered why cats have whiskers? Or maybe you've asked why our cheeks get all warm and red when we get embarrassed. Or perhaps you've asked what it's called when a big tornado mixes with a blazing wildfire (spoiler alert: it's a firenado!). For all the questions you wonder about, there is Someone who knows every answer—God! He made everything on this planet and in all the galaxies, and here's the most amazing part: He invites us to ask all of our questions and to uncover the wonder of creation!

These pages are filled with 100 mind-blowing and fun-filled devotions about the beauty God intentionally created throughout the universe. We could write a zillion devotions about God, and it wouldn't even scratch the surface of how wonder-full He truly is. As much as we continue to discover about space, earth, animals, and people, there are still endless treasures to find! From rushing waterfalls to crashing waves, and from mountain peaks to the green grasses of the prairies, everything God made is overflowing with wonder and shows us how great He is!

I've invited back some amazing and trusted friends to join us on our journey. Meet six kids who are exploring and growing just like you: Evyn, Raz, Norah, Joshua, Clarke, and Adelynn.

Throughout this book, we'll focus our minds and hearts on learning about what God has made by reading about different parts of His creation, digging into amazing science facts, talking with Him in prayer, and growing deeper in knowledge to understand His brilliance. My hope for you is that as you dive into these pages, you would see the inspiring connection between the world around you and the God who created it.

If you'd like to focus on a specific part of creation, feel free to jump around this book! We'll talk about four main topics; you can find them on these pages:

Space: pages 14, 22, 30, 38, 54, 62, 70, 78, 86, 94, 102, 110, 118, 126, 132, 134, 142, 152, 160, 168, 176, 182, 184, 196, 204

Earth: pages 6, 12, 20, 28, 32, 36, 44, 52, 60, 68, 76, 84, 92, 100, 108, 116, 124, 150, 158, 166, 180, 188, 192, 194, 202

Animals: pages 10, 26, 34, 42, 50, 58, 66, 74, 82, 90, 98, 104, 106, 114, 122, 130, 138, 140, 148, 156, 164, 172, 178, 186, 200

People: pages 8, 16, 18, 24, 40, 46, 48, 56, 64, 72, 80, 88, 96, 112, 120, 128, 136, 144, 146, 154, 162, 170, 174, 190, 198

I'm so glad that you have joined me for this exploration. As we get ready to take off, prepare to have your minds blown and your eyes opened to this truth: God has woven amazing wonder into all of creation. So let's begin discovering it.

Enjoy the adventure ahead!

Pastor Louie

GET A LiTTLE CLOSER

Jesus opened their minds so they
could understand the Scriptures.

LUKE 24:45 ICB

Some scientists say we know more about the surface of Mars than about the bottom of the oceans. But the National Oceanic and Atmospheric Administration—NOAA for short—is working to change that.

6

In 2009, NOAA launched the *Okeanos Explorer* ship to map and explore the ocean floor. A remote-control vehicle named *Deep Discoverer* dives down to 19,000 feet underwater. (That's over 3½ miles down!) Along the way, it takes pictures, collects samples, and discovers creatures like the *Duobrachium sparksae* (a new species of comb jelly) and a "ghost-like" octopod no one has ever seen before!

Each year, *Okeanos* maps between 23,000 and 38,000 square miles. But since the ocean is over 139,000,000 square miles, they've still got a lot of ground . . . I mean . . . water to cover. Space satellites can give us a rough outline of what's down there. But to fill in the details, explorers need to dive in and get a little closer.

That's true about God too. If we just "look" at Him during church once a week, we

Are there lilies under the sea? Sort of. These "flowers" bloomed years and years ago, when volcanic activity in the Gulf of Mexico forced streams of thick tar up through cracks in the ocean floor—kind of like squeezing Play-Doh through your fingers. As the tar cooled in the water, it took the shape of huge flower petals, so scientists called them "tar lilies."

can learn some things about who He is. And that's great! But to fill in the details, we to need to dive into His Word and get a little closer. That means looking up words we don't know, asking for help with verses we don't understand, and talking to God about what it all means. When you set out to discover more about God, you'll meet the One who's more amazing than anything you could discover here on Earth—even at the bottom of the ocean.

God, I want to deeply know You. Help me fill in the details and understand what I read in Your Word. Amen.

7

A PLAN AND A PURPOSE

The LORD will work out his plans for my life.

PSALM 138:8 NLT

This might sound gross, but did you know that there's this little worm-like pouch inside your body? It's about two to four inches long, and scientists had no idea why it's there—until recently. That little pouch is called the appendix (uh-PEN-diks). It's attached to your large intestine, which is attached to your small intestine (which is 22 feet long and not all that small), which is attached to your stomach. *Whew!*

Those organs all work together to digest your food—except the appendix. For years, scientists believed the appendix had no real purpose. But now they believe it's actually pretty important. It stores good bacteria (not the bad kind that makes you sick), which is important because your digestive system needs good bacteria to break down your food. But when you get sick, especially with a stomachache, the good bacteria can get flushed out of your system. That's when the appendix comes to the rescue! It releases the stored up good bacteria and gets your digestive system back on track!

Okay, let's think about this. If God has an important purpose for even that tiny, worm-like pouch in your belly, just imagine what He's got planned for your whole body! God created you and put you in this time and place for a reason. And He's going to use everything that happens in your life—yes, even the things that don't seem to have a purpose right now—to help you grow and learn and be able to carry out His plan for you. Some days, it might be hard to see, but never doubt that God's got a plan and a purpose created just for you!

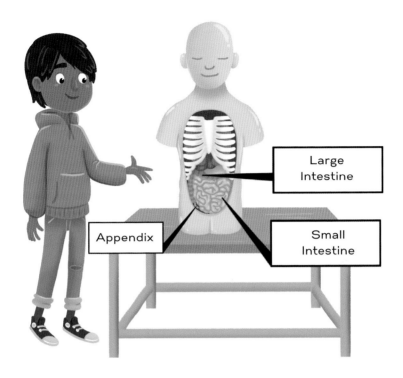

Large Intestine

Appendix

Small Intestine

Lord, I know You have good plans for me—plans that will show off just how awesome You are. Please direct me in the next step to take. Amen.

EXPLORE THE WONDER

Ever wonder how food gets through your digestive system? Muscle power! Waves of muscle movement—kind of like the waves in the ocean—push food down your esophagus, into the stomach, and then through the intestines. It's called peristalsis (per-uh-STAL-sis). Since it uses muscle power instead of gravity, you could digest your food standing on your head!

LOST AND FOUND

God is being patient with you. He does not want anyone to
be lost. He wants everyone to change his heart and life.

2 PETER 3:9 ICB

No one had seen a Somali sengi since 1973. *What's a Somali sengi?* you ask. It's a species of elephant shrew. Yeah, it's mouse-sized, but it really *is* related to the elephant—just check out its extra-long nose!

For almost 50 years, scientists believed the Somali sengi was extinct. But they kept hearing rumors about sengis being spotted in the rocky lands of

Djibouti in Africa. So, in 2019, scientists set out over 1,200 traps to find them. For bait, they used a mixture of peanut butter, oatmeal, and yeast. Turns out, sengis love peanut butter! Scientists caught—and safely released—12 Somali sengis. The animal everyone thought was lost had been found.

Scientists didn't want the Somali sengi to be lost, and God doesn't want you or anyone else to be lost either. This isn't "lost" like being lost in a city. This "lost" means a person hasn't trusted God to be the Lord of their life. That's why God never stops searching for us and chasing after us with His love. Sometimes it's in big ways, like sending Jesus to save us from sin. And other times it's in smaller ways, like sending a friend to remind us how much God loves us.

God never gives up on anyone—not the nosy neighbor, the pizza delivery guy, or that mean kid on the bus, and definitely not you. He's always working, searching, and chasing because He wants absolutely everyone to be found and to follow Him!

God, I want to be more like You. Help me to never stop showing the world how much You love everyone in it. Amen.

EXPLORE THE WONDER

What is it about teeny-tiny animals that makes them impossible to resist? Like the Baluchistan pygmy jerboa (also known as the dwarf three-toed jerboa). These little guys hop around the deserts of Pakistan like little kangaroos. It's the world's smallest rodent, with a less-than-two-inch-long body and a three-inch-long tail. And it weighs barely more than a penny!

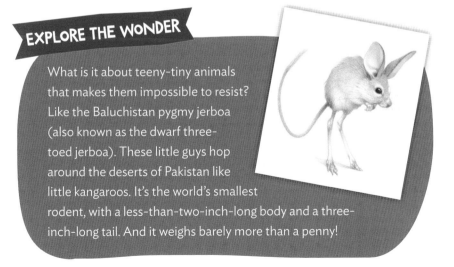

FIRENADO

"Don't be afraid. I am with you."

ISAIAH 43:5 ICB

All of us would agree that a sudden and unexpected wildfire **is bad.** We would agree that a tornado is definitely bad. But put them together? That's when bad goes to worse—and it's called a firenado!

Firenadoes are huge, twisting towers of fire. While tornadoes form in the sky, firenadoes form closer to the ground. As the hot, dry air of a wildfire rises, the air sometimes starts to spin. As it does, it can pick up not only dirt and sticks but also fire, creating a firenado!

Firenadoes can range from just a few inches wide to over 500 feet wide. They usually last only a few minutes, but one of the largest recorded firenadoes lasted almost an hour and stretched 18,000 feet into the air! Firenadoes spew sparks in every direction, so they're incredibly dangerous for firefighters.

When bad goes to worse in your world, you might ask, "Where is God?" The answer is that He's with you—even in the fire! Check out the story of Shadrach, Meshach, and Abednego (Daniel 3). The king ordered them to bow down and worship a golden statue, but they refused. They would only worship God. So the king had them thrown into a fiery furnace as punishment. But when the king looked at the fire, he saw *four* men, not three, walking inside the furnace. God didn't leave Shadrach, Meshach, and Abednego alone in that fire. And when they came out, they didn't even smell like smoke!

When bad goes to worse in your world, remember Shadrach, Meshach, and Abednego—and know that God will be with you in the fire too!

God, even when bad goes to worse and I feel like fire is surrounding me, I know You are with me. I will trust You to protect me through the fire. Amen.

It's raining . . . fish? It did in Tampico, Mexico, in 2017. During a rain shower, small fish also fell to the ground. And in 2005, in the town of Odzaci in Serbia, it rained frogs! Why are fish and frogs falling from the sky? Scientists think they may have been sucked up by a passing tornado or hurricane. Then, when the storm lost its strength, the fish and frogs "rained" down.

DRIFTING AWAY

"When you search for me with all
your heart, you will find me!"

JEREMIAH 29:13 ICB

Earth isn't the only planet in our solar system that has a moon. In fact, all the major planets in our solar system have moons, except Mercury and Venus. Saturn even has 82 moons! And one of them—Titan—is drifting away. There's no need to worry, though. That's just what moons do.

Astronomers knew Titan was getting farther and farther away from Saturn. It's just happening much faster than they thought. It's zipping away a whole four inches every single year. Okay, so that's not really *zipping*, especially since Titan is already 759,000 *miles* away from Saturn.

How did astronomers figure out how fast Titan was drifting? The spacecraft *Cassini* spent 13 years orbiting (or circling) Saturn, and it sent back lots of photos and information about Titan while it was "in the neighborhood." The fact that Titan is drifting faster than scientists thought means that our whole solar system may have been created much faster than they thought—like in an instant when "God created the heavens and the earth" (Genesis 1:1 NIV).

While Titan's drifting away isn't anything to worry about, drifting away from God is. And it can happen so easily! It might start with something tiny, like skipping your Bible reading or prayers on a day when you're busy. But then that one day stretches into two or three days, then a week, and then you don't remember the last time you just sat with God and His Word. But unlike moons, we can zip right back to God. When we search for Him, we find Him! Start with a prayer, then dive into the Bible. He's waiting for you there!

God, show me when I start to drift away from You, and then help me come zipping back to You. Amen.

EXPLORE THE WONDER

Earth's Moon is drifting away too, but not nearly as fast as Titan. Our Moon is only slipping about 1 to $1\frac{1}{2}$ inches away each year. Since it's already 238,855 miles away, scientists believe we'll be enjoying moon-filled nights for a few billion years to come.

STRESSED OUT!

Do not be interested only in your own life,
but be interested in the lives of others.

PHILIPPIANS 2:4 ICB

S **tress!** You've probably heard that word once or twice—or maybe a zillion times. That's because every person—no matter how old they are—has stress in their life. So, what is stress? Stress is the way your body

reacts to what you're thinking and feeling. It actually starts in your brain. When you feel worried, nervous, upset, afraid, or angry about something, your brain sends out a message to your body: "Hey, I'm feeling a little stressed here!" That's when your body starts its "stress response."

Everyone's stress response is a little different. Your hands might sweat and shake. Or you might get a stomachache. Your heart might beat faster, you might have trouble sleeping, or your voice might shake when you speak. When you're stressed, take a big, deep, slow breath. Then maybe a few more. Next, take a look around and figure out what's causing the stress. Is it a big test? Is it tryouts for the team? Is it heading off to camp on your own? If there's something you can do about it, then do it. Study, practice, or pack extra bug spray. Then stop thinking about yourself and shift your focus to other people.

If you're feeling extra stressed, try getting some exercise. Scientists have found that when we exercise, our bodies create endorphins (en-DAWR-finz). They send a message to your brain that says, "Hey, I'm feeling pretty good!" So when stress zaps you, get up and dance or go for a run—and grab a friend to join in on the fun!

For example, if you're nervous about heading off to that new camp, chances are there is someone else who's stressed about the very same thing. Decide to encourage them. Smile, say hello, and be a friend. When you think about others instead of yourself, you soon find that you feel much better— and you've helped someone else! Jesus would call it being "interested in the lives of others." And it's something He did a lot of too!

Lord, teach me to spend less time thinking about myself and spend more time thinking about other people. Amen.

LEAD THE WAY!

"The greatest among you must be a servant."

MATTHEW 23:11 NLT

Climbing to the top of Mount Everest, one of the tallest mountains in the world, takes weeks of being out in the ice and snow. There are falling rocks, avalanches, 200-mile-an-hour winds, and jumping spiders! *What?!* The climb is incredibly difficult to navigate, and there are no "walk this way" signs to help you. So how do you get to the top? You need someone to lead the way. You need a Sherpa!

Sherpas are people who live in the mountainous region of Nepal near Mount Everest. (We say *SHER-puh*, but the Sherpa people say *SHER-wa*). They're known for their epic climbing skills. Not only do they know which path to take up the mountain, but they also know what you'll need to get there—and they'll even help you carry it.

The Sherpas haven't always climbed mountains, though. In fact, they started out farming, raising cattle, and spinning wool. But when people began climbing Mount Everest, Sherpas were hired to lead the way because they knew the area. The Sherpas *learned* to be leaders. And you can too.

To be a great leader, remember this: Leading isn't about being the boss or telling everyone what to do. It's about helping others find their way. That might mean showing a new kid how to find the lunchroom and inviting them to your table, helping an old friend figure out how to tell their parents they messed up, or pointing someone to Jesus.

Jesus came to lead us all the way home to heaven, but He did it by helping and serving the people around Him. Let's follow His example and learn to be leaders who serve.

God, I want to be like Jesus and lead others to You. Show me who I can serve today and how I can help them find their way. Amen.

EXPLORE THE WONDER

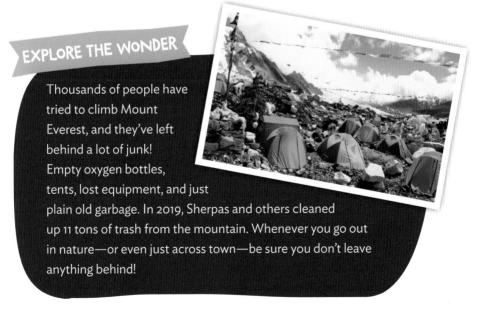

Thousands of people have tried to climb Mount Everest, and they've left behind a lot of junk! Empty oxygen bottles, tents, lost equipment, and just plain old garbage. In 2019, Sherpas and others cleaned up 11 tons of trash from the mountain. Whenever you go out in nature—or even just across town—be sure you don't leave anything behind!

WORDS ON THE WEB

I hope my words and thoughts please you.
Lord, you are my Rock, the one who saves me.

PSALM 19:14 ICB

J ump on the web. Surf the internet. You hear those phrases a lot these days, so you might think the web and the internet are the same thing— but they're not.

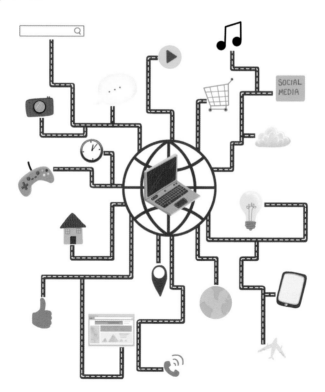

The internet is a network of computers all linked together, mostly using telephone lines. It's like a bunch of roads that zigzag all over the world and connect all the different places to each other. Things like the World Wide Web, emails, and text messages are like cars that travel along the internet's roads, carrying different kinds of information. Digital downloads (like movies and music) are another connection, and so are video calls with your teacher or friends.

One of the most popular ways of moving information around the internet is social media. You can use that technology to connect with friends near and far, but be careful! Talk to your parents before using social media. And if you're allowed to use it, ask them for safety rules—like never share your address or phone number, don't connect with people you don't know, and always think before you post. Why? Because it's so easy to type something that you'd *never* say to someone's face. When you post something online, it's like putting up a giant billboard for the world to see. *Forever.* Because nothing ever really goes away on the internet, even if you delete it. Remember, when the Bible tells us to be careful with our words, it means the words we type too!

God, help me to always choose my words carefully, whether I'm talking to someone in person or posting on the web. Amen.

NOW YOU SEE IT

Two people are better than one. They get more done by working together.

ECCLESIASTES 4:9 ICB

People said it couldn't be done. But astronomers—scientists who study space—from around the world began working together, and they did it! They took a picture of a black hole! It's in a galaxy called M87, which is 53 million light-years away. (Just one light-year is 5,880,000,000,000 miles!)

Black holes are mysterious places in space that form when a star dies. The gravity, or pull, of a black hole is really strong. It's so strong that if anything gets too close, it gets sucked right in. Not even light can escape! That's what makes a black hole completely, well, *black*—and invisible in the darkness of

First horizon-scale image of a black hole in the center of galaxy M87

space. It's tough to take a picture of something invisible. So astronomers took a picture of hot, glowing gas getting sucked into the black hole. One camera couldn't do that job by itself. It took a bunch of telescopes working together to capture this amazing picture. The black center inside the ring of glowing gases is the black hole!

By working together, astronomers did something no one had done before. God has given you special talents, and you can use them to do some amazing things for God. But when you work together with others, you can do even bigger things that help more people learn about God. Things like putting on an entire Bible story play for younger kids, having a service day to help elderly people with yard work, or going caroling at a nursing home (whether it's Christmas or not). When we work together for God, wonderful things happen!

God, more can be done for Your name by working together than working alone. Teach me how to work well with others so even more people will learn about You. Amen.

EXPLORE THE WONDER

On October 24, 1946, soldiers and scientists worked together to launch a missile that carried a motion picture camera. It took pictures from 65 miles above the Earth—the edge of outer space. The camera was wrapped in a steel case to keep it safe as it crashed back to Earth. When scientists checked the film, they saw Earth from space for the first time ever!

UNDER ATTACK!

The Lord is faithful. He will give you strength
and protect you from the Evil One.

2 THESSALONIANS 3:3 ICB

A **aa-choo!** Ever wonder why we get colds? Blame it on a kind of germ
called a virus (VI-ruhs). Viruses can't live long outside of our bodies,
so their mission is to get inside of us. Once inside, the virus attaches to a
cell. It actually sort of kidnaps that cell. Then it injects instructions into the
cell that force it to make copies of the virus. Those copies then head out
and take over more cells. Basically, viruses are like a gang of microscopic
bad guys.

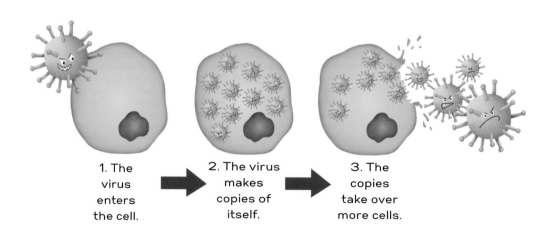

1. The virus enters the cell.

2. The virus makes copies of itself.

3. The copies take over more cells.

But God gave our bodies a whole army of white blood cells whose job is to fight off viruses and other germs. They're constantly on the alert, looking for invaders. When they spot one, they destroy it with weapons called antibodies (AN-ti-bod-eez). When all the invaders are gone, the "army" goes back to resting—except for a few memory cells. They "remember" that particular invader and are constantly searching for it. If it shows up again, they can zap it so fast we might not even know we were sick!

Germs aren't the only things attacking us, though. The devil does too. He attacks with troubles, bad days, and temptations, hoping we'll do the wrong thing. But God gave us a way to fight off his attacks. It's called prayer, and it's the most powerful weapon ever. When you pray, God hears you and comes to fight for you. And then—like memory cells—you have the memories of how God helped you in the past to remind you that God will help you again!

Lord, thank You for Your faithfulness, and for all the ways You protect me and help me stay strong. Amen.

Y-shaped antibodies attacking a virus and protecting a cell

Have you heard about "herd immunity"? Here's a hint: it has nothing to do with cows. Instead, when someone gets sick from a virus and their body fights it off, they become immune (ih-MYOON) to that virus. That means they can't get sick from that virus again. When most of the people in a community are immune, it's called herd immunity.

IT ALL ADDS UP

Trust the Lord and do good.

PSALM 37:3 ICB

Have you ever heard the saying "as busy as a beaver"? People associate beavers with busyness for a good reason—these guys are always working on their dams. With powerful jaws and super-strong teeth, they "chop" down trees and cut up branches. Then they drag the wood into the water, float it over to the building site, and pack it all together with mud to build a dam. The dam causes the water to pool together into a deep, still pond. Beavers dive into the pond to escape predators—like coyotes, wolves, bears, and eagles. They live in a domed lodge on top of the dam. These lodges usually have an underwater entrance and two dens—one for drying off and one for living in. Pretty clever, huh?

With sticks and mud, beavers can completely change their environment, turning a forest or meadow into a pond. Which proves that little things really

do make a big difference. Kind of like good habits, which are those little things we do every day without thinking much about them. Maybe it's reading the Bible every morning, saying a bedtime prayer, picking up litter whenever you see it, or doing at least one nice thing for someone every day. Maybe you think those "little" habits don't make a difference, but they do. They help us remember to talk to God and to take care of His people and His creation every day. And they all add up to make a huge difference in our world. So, what "little" habit can you start today?

Lord, what little thing can I do today to make a big difference in my life and the world around me? Amen.

EXPLORE THE WONDER

In France in 1879, postman Ferdinand Cheval spotted a rock so interesting that he put it in his pocket and took it home.
That rock was the first of many he picked up over the next 33 years. He used them to build the *Palais Idéal du Facteur Cheval*. That's French for *The Ideal Palace of the Postman Cheval*. It has stone giants, dozens of animals, and even its own waterfall!

SOOO SLOW!

"I will put a new spirit in them. I will
take away that heart of stone, and I
will put a real heart in its place."

EZEKIEL 11:19 ERV

Imagine seeing nothing around you but massive sheets of ice!
Brrr! That's exactly what you'll find in parts of Alaska, Greenland, and
other places. They're called glaciers (GLEY-sherz), and they can stretch out
for miles. Glaciers are masses of snow and ice that form where the snow falls

faster than it can melt. Over hundreds of years, all that snow is pressed together into slabs that can be more than 1,500 feet thick.

You might not know it, but glaciers actually move. Gravity pulls them down the mountains. But don't expect to see one zooming by—if you think turtles move slow, check out the speed of a glacier. Some only move an inch or two a day. The fastest moving one is in Greenland, and it moves less than eight miles a year. If you were to drive that "fast" across the US, it would take about 365 years!

Glaciers move pretty slow, but sometimes hearts can seem to move even slower. I don't mean how fast they beat; I'm talking about how they change. Maybe you've been smiling at that grouchy neighbor for weeks and still haven't gotten a smile back. Or you say hello to that grumpy kid on the bus every day, and he still won't say hi back. Or maybe you've been telling your friend about Jesus for ages, but she still won't come to church. Don't give up. Don't stop loving or caring or trying. God is using your kindness to move and change other people's hearts—even when it's happening slower than a glacier moves.

Lord, I know Your love can move mountains. Help me trust that You are working even if I don't see anything change around me. Amen.

A SOFT LANDING

If they stumble, they will not fall,
because the LORD holds their hand.

PSALM 37:24 NCV

Imagine hurtling toward the surface of Mars at almost 950 mph (miles per hour). That's faster than the speed of sound! It looks like it will be a crash landing, but seconds later—*whoosh!*—your parachute pops out and slows your fall to a gentle 200 mph. Rocket thrusters guide you the rest of the way down to a soft landing. Sound crazy? That's exactly what happened when the Perseverance (pur-suh-VEER-uhns) rover landed on Mars in February of 2021 (check out page 132).

Perseverance's parachute was the biggest one ever used for a Mars mission. It was 70.5 feet wide, or as long as two buses parked end to end. This special space parachute was made of light but extra-strong nylon, Technora (stronger than steel!), and Kevlar (the stuff used to make bulletproof vests). The parachute worked by "catching" the air and slowing down Perseverance's fall. Because there's so little air to "catch" on Mars, small rocket thrusters slowed the fall even more to give the rover a soft landing.

NASA's Perseverance Mars Rover

Do you ever feel like you're falling and about to crash? Maybe it's when you study your hardest and still bomb the test, or when your parents are fighting over and over again. Trust God to give you a soft landing. That might mean that your problem gets fixed and disappears. Or it might mean that God helps you get through it. His "parachute" might look like a shoulder to lean on, a note from a friend, or a Bible verse that He slips into your day. When you feel like you're about to crash, keep holding on to Him, and He'll help you land softly.

God, thank You for always being there to catch me when I fall and feel like I'm about to crash. Amen.

EXPLORE THE WONDER

Leonardo da Vinci sketched out the *idea* of a parachute way back in the 1470s. But it was André-Jacques Garnerin who tested the first modern parachute in France in 1797. He attached the parachute to a basket and a hot-air balloon—and then climbed in! When he was more than half a mile above the ground, he cut the balloon free and parachuted to the ground. It was a bumpy landing, but he lived! A couple of years later, his wife, Jeanne-Geneviève, became the first woman to jump with a parachute.

THE CHOCOLATE HiLLS

Everything God created is good.

1 TIMOTHY 4:4 NIV

Stare too long at the hills in Bohol Province of the Philippines, and you just might get a craving for chocolate. That's because in winter, when the grasses turn brown, these hills look like mile after mile of gigantic chocolate drops. Which is why they're called the Chocolate Hills.

Sadly, they aren't really made of chocolate. Instead, they're made of marine limestone. Marine limestone is rock that was once under the ocean's waters. Even now, the hills are filled with the fossils of coral, algae, and mollusks

(a family of animals that includes clams, snails, and squid). Scientists aren't 100 percent sure how the hills were formed. But at least 1,260 of these yummy-looking hills are spread out over 20 square miles. Most hills are between 98 and 164 feet tall, but the largest is at least 390 feet tall! (That's like having you and 85 of your closest friends all stacked on top of each other.)

While scientists might not be exactly sure how the hills were formed, I've got a theory: it's because chocolate hills are fun to make. You see, God is a creator. That means that He gets creative, and sometimes it's just for fun. (I mean, have you seen a giraffe?) God made you to be creative too. So when you use your imagination to make something—something that wasn't there before—you're doing what God made you to do, and that is a kind of worship! Create something for Him today. You can even use chocolate if you want to.

God, thank You for the gift of creativity and imagination. Teach me how to use these gifts to worship You. Amen.

EXPLORE THE WONDER

Create something. Just for fun. It could be a painting, a story, a song, a yummy cake, or a new way to solve that math problem. Don't worry about making it perfect or for anyone to see. Do it because you want to and because it's fun. Create because God the Creator made you to create things too.

WASH IT CLEAN!

Wash away all my guilt and
make me clean again.

PSALM 51:2 ICB

If people say you eat like a pig, it's probably not a compliment! Unless they're comparing you to one of the European boars found in a Switzerland zoo. These picky pigs prefer to wash their food before they eat it. Zookeepers even tested them by giving them a pile of cut-up apples to eat, and the pigs gobbled the clean apples right up! But if the apples landed in the dirt, the pigs dropped them in a nearby creek to rinse them off first. In this case, eating like a pig doesn't sound *so* bad!

When it comes to apples, washing the outside is good enough. But when it comes to people, we need to wash the inside too. Because if we don't clean our hearts, we'll be like the Pharisees in the Bible. On the outside they *looked* like they were doing everything God wanted. But on the inside, they were filthy with pride, greed, and selfishness (Luke 11:39). If we're not careful, we can be the same way—looking good on the outside, while on the inside we're feeling jealous or thinking something mean.

To wash our insides, we need Jesus' help. First, we have to confess. That means telling Jesus about any wrong things we've done or said or thought, like lying to a teacher or thinking mean thoughts about a sibling. Next, we ask Him to forgive us. And then, we ask Jesus to fill us up with His goodness instead. Then we'll be clean, inside and out!

God, forgive me for the wrong things I do and for when I look good on the outside but am messy on the inside. Clean my heart and mind so the whole world will know I love You. Amen.

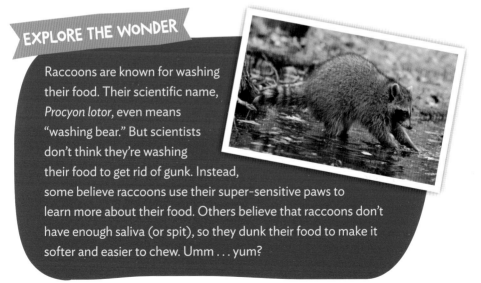

EXPLORE THE WONDER

Raccoons are known for washing their food. Their scientific name, *Procyon lotor*, even means "washing bear." But scientists don't think they're washing their food to get rid of gunk. Instead, some believe raccoons use their super-sensitive paws to learn more about their food. Others believe that raccoons don't have enough saliva (or spit), so they dunk their food to make it softer and easier to chew. Umm . . . yum?

TAKING CARE OF THE WORLD

We are workers together with God.

2 CORINTHIANS 6:1 ICB

I magine a land filled with elephants, chimpanzees, gorillas, hippos, leopards, lions, and hundreds of other animals. Over 1,000 species of birds flutter through the air, and over 10,000 different tropical plants grow here. The land is rich with rubber, timber, copper, diamonds, tin, and gold. And over 75 million people call this area home. What is this amazing place? The Congo Basin in Africa.

The Congo Basin is the area of land surrounding the Congo River, which is the world's deepest river. At 720 feet deep, you could stack two Statues of

Liberty on top of each other and still be underwater! The river is 2,920 miles long and crosses the equator twice. All that water so close to the hot, hot, hot temperatures of the equator creates the perfect environment for the world's second largest rainforest. (The Amazon rainforest holds the number-one spot!)

But the Congo Basin is in danger. Poachers are killing too many animals, the rainforest is being cut down, and the frequent wars aren't helping anyone.

God told us to take care of the Earth—even those parts halfway around the world (Genesis 2:15). How can you help the Congo? One way has to do with the foods grown in and near rainforests—foods like bananas and cocoa. Ask your parents to look for foods that are sustainably grown. That means the farming doesn't hurt the forests. Little things can make a big difference when you work with those around you and with God to make the world a cleaner, happier place.

God, show me what I can do today to make this world a better and more beautiful place. Amen.

Imagine how this world must have been when God first made it. What can you do to make it more like that again? Think small: pick up a piece of trash. Think a little bigger: plant a tree. Think, dream, and plan *really* big: maybe you start a community garden or a recycling program at church or school. What can you do to take care of God's creation?

A CASE OF MISTAKEN IDENTITY

"But what about you?" [Jesus]
asked. "Who do you say I am?"

MATTHEW 16:15 NIV

*O**ops!** I thought you were someone else!* It's so embarrassing when you see someone you think you know and tap them on the shoulder—but when they turn around, they're not who you thought they were. Something like that happened to astronomers and the dwarf planet Ceres (SEE-reez).

Ceres was discovered back in 1801 by an astronomer named Giuseppe Piazzi. When he first saw Ceres tucked in between Mars and Jupiter, he thought it was a comet. But when he talked to other astronomers, they decided it was a planet. In 1802, another astronomer called it an asteroid. Over 200 years later, in 2006, astronomers changed their minds again and said Ceres was a dwarf planet. *Whew!* Talk about a case of mistaken identity!

Jesus knows all about the problem of mistaken identity. People can get really confused about who He is. Some say He was a good man, a prophet, or an amazing teacher. Others say He was crazy to claim He is the Son of God. But when Jesus asked Peter, "Who do you say I am?" Peter knew the answer: "You are the Christ, the Son of the living God" (Matthew 16:16 ICB).

Dig in and discover for yourself who Jesus is. Because personally knowing who Jesus is—the Son of God—is what matters most. Read the Bible, look at all He said and did, and ask God to show you the truth. When you do, there's no mistaking His identity!

God, guide me as I read Your Word. Show me who Jesus really is. Help me see and believe that He is Your Son. Amen.

EXPLORE THE WONDER

So far, astronomers have discovered five dwarf planets in our solar system: Pluto, Makemake, Haumea, Eris, and Ceres. Pluto is probably the best-known dwarf planet. (Astronomers thought it was a planet until 2006.) But Ceres is the first to get its very own visit from a spacecraft. The *Dawn* orbiter launched in 2007 and—after a visit to Vesta, the brightest asteroid in the sky—it arrived at Ceres in 2015.

DON'T SHARE!

Love is not rude, is not selfish, and
does not become angry easily.

1 CORINTHIANS 13:5 ICB

*D*on't share? That sounds like the worst advice ever, right? Well, that depends on what you're sharing. Sharing your friendship, a smile, or a plate of homemade cookies is awesome. But sharing nasty germs that can make us sick? That's definitely not awesome.

One of the easiest ways to avoid sharing germs is to cover your mouth because coughing or sneezing into the air sends tiny water drops flying everywhere. Just one cough can shoot out 3,000 drops, while a sneeze might have 40,000! And one little drop is packed with germs that can hang out in the air for *hours*. Those germs can also live on things like doorknobs, tablets, and remote controls for up to 24 hours or even longer! So cover your mouth with a tissue, or cough or sneeze into your elbow instead.

Germs aren't the only things we shouldn't share. Grumpy, bad attitudes are another. Sure, we all have them once in a while. Maybe we had a fight with a friend, or it's just been a lousy day. It's okay to be upset when things go wrong. But it's not okay to be rude, hateful, or just plain unpleasant to be around. Talk it out with God, a parent, or a friend. Take a deep breath and think of something good that happened in your day instead. But make sure the spread of grumpiness stops with you.

To see how germs spread, try this experiment: Grab four slices of bread. Cough on one slice of bread. Rub a second slice over your hands. Rub a third slice over a phone screen or countertop. Do nothing to the fourth piece. Put each slice in a separate baggie. Use a spray bottle to spray a little water in each bag. Label and seal the bags. Keep in a warm, dark place for a week. How did the germs spread?

Lord, when I'm having a bad day, thank You for listening to my troubles. Help me not to share my grumpiness with other people and make sure the bad attitude ends with me. Amen.

BEHIND THE SCENES

"Your Father can see what is done in
secret, and he will reward you."

MATTHEW 6:4 ICB

There's no goofing off if you're an ant. Every *single* ant in a colony has a job to do, even if you can't see it. There's the queen, who lays eggs. There are the drones, who stay with the queen. And finally, there are the workers. They're the smallest ants, but they do most of the work, which explains their name. The worker ants take care of the eggs, pupae, and larvae

(sort of like baby ants). They also take out the trash, find food, and defend the nest against invaders. Some workers stay so busy they never leave the nest. They may not be the biggest or strongest, but without their behind-the-scenes work, the colony wouldn't survive.

That reminds me of Obadiah in 1 Kings 18. If you haven't heard of Obadiah, that's totally okay. Lots of people haven't. He lived in Old Testament times and worked behind the scenes to save a bunch of God's prophets from an evil queen. So you might not know his name, but God definitely does!

Doing important things for God means more than just the stuff everybody can see—like preaching, leading prayers, or being a missionary in a faraway land. Those are all great, but so are all the behind-the-scenes things. Like sending a card to that faraway missionary, teaching a younger kid a Bible song, or saying a little prayer for someone who's having a rough day. It doesn't matter whether or not the whole world knows, because God sees every little thing you do—even behind the scenes.

Lord, help me remember that every single thing I do for You is important—whether anybody knows about it or not. Amen.

SHARE THE WONDER

You can do important things for God! Think of at least one kind and helpful thing you can do secretly for someone every day this week. Slip a Bible verse in your mom's purse or tape it to the fridge. Make a snack for your brother or sister. Say a prayer for a hurting friend. Be a behind-the-scenes worker for God today!

THE RiNG oF FiRE

Look for peace and work for it.

1 PETER 3:11 ICB

Have you ever met a really big guy named Tiny? Or munched on a "jumbo" shrimp? Sometimes names just don't fit. Like *Pacific Ocean*. *Pacific* means "peaceful," but these ocean waters are anything but! They're home to the Ring of Fire—as in *452 volcanoes* kind of fire. The Ring of Fire makes up 75 percent of the world's volcanic activity. And it causes about 90 percent of the Earth's earthquakes.

The Ring of Fire isn't actually a ring, though. It's more of a crooked horseshoe shape. It stretches from South America to Alaska. Then it heads over toward

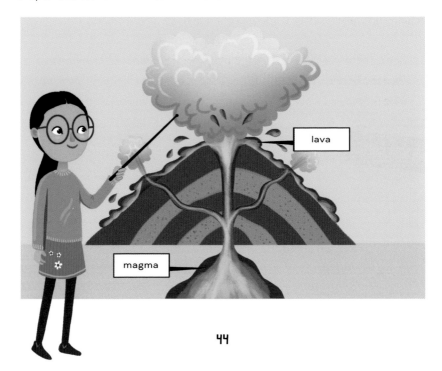

Russia and Japan and down to New Zealand before ending up in Antarctica. That's more than 24,900 miles long!

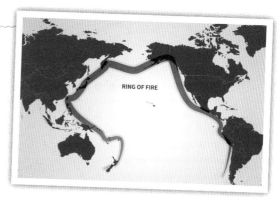

RING OF FIRE

What makes the Ring of Fire so fiery? Gigantic tectonic (tek-TON-ik) plates float along under the Earth's surface on a layer of melted rock called magma. Sometimes those plates bump and rub against each other. That's when things can get really interesting, if not explosive!

Just like two tectonic plates rubbing against each other, you'll encounter people who rub you the wrong way. And just like with those tectonic plates, the tension can get explosive. But God wants us to be peacemakers and cool things down. That means being patient, kind, and forgiving. It means letting go of your anger and choosing not to get even. And sometimes, it means simply smiling and walking away. Look for a chance to be a peacemaker today!

Lord, there are times when I get so angry, I just want to get even. Please give me the wisdom to be loving and patient instead. Show me how to be a peacemaker—even if there's chaos around me. Amen.

EXPLORE THE WONDER

The Moon has its share of earthquakes, or *moonquakes*, too. Scientists think the quakes that happen deep under the Moon's surface may be caused by the pull of Earth's gravity. But quakes closer to the surface are probably caused by meteoroids hitting the Moon or by the huge temperature changes—from 250 degrees Fahrenheit in the day to -208 degrees in the darkness, or even colder!

WiGGLE YOUR EARS?

We all have different gifts. Each gift came
because of the grace that God gave us.

ROMANS 12:6 ICB

You can wiggle your fingers. You can wiggle your toes. And chances
are, you can probably wiggle your nose. But can you wiggle your ears?
Some people can, and some people can't, no matter how hard they try!

The secret is in being able to control a small group of muscles behind your ears called the auriculares (oh-rik-yuh-LAR-eez). One of these muscles pulls the ear forward, another pulls it up, and the third pulls it backward. But only about 10 to 20 people out of every 100 can do it.

The fact is, other people can do things that we'll never be able to do, no matter how hard we try. I'm not ever going to be a prima ballerina. There's just no way I could ever stand on my toes like that. And I'm not ever going to be a world-famous opera singer because I can't hit those high notes. Those just aren't the gifts God gave me. And you know what? That's okay. Because God made me to be amazing at other things. And He made you to be amazing in your own way too.

Don't beat yourself up because someone can do something you can't. Cheer them on, then go figure out what you're really great at. Experiment. Try new things. It's okay if it doesn't work out; try something else. God has given each of us different talents and gifts. Figure out what yours are. Then use them to help others and to show how awesome He is.

God, help me figure out what gifts You've given me—and how to use them to tell the world how wonderful You are. Amen.

EXPLORE THE WONDER

The prize for world's largest ears goes to the African elephant. Their massive ears can grow to be six feet long and four feet wide. Each ear is filled with thousands of tiny blood vessels that pull extra heat away from their body to help keep them cool. And those big floppy ears make pretty good fans too!

FiGHT oR FLiGHT?

I will not be afraid because you are with me.

PSALM 23:4 ICB

"**B** oo!" your little brother yells as he jumps out from behind a door. You flinch in surprise. He falls on the floor laughing, but not you. You're ready to sock him, run away, or both! What's happening? That *boo* triggered your body's fight-or-flight response.

When you get scared, your body gets ready to either *fight* off whatever scared you—or run away as fast as you can (*flight*). So, your heart pumps extra blood to your muscles and brain. You breathe faster to get more oxygen into your body. And the pupils in your eyes get bigger, or dilate (DIE-layt), to help you see better. All this happens so you can think better, move faster, and see the danger that's coming at you. Your stomach even stops digesting, and you might even wet yourself. Don't worry! That's just because your body is choosing to focus on the fight or flight instead.

God gave us the fight-or-flight response to help us when we're threatened. He also gave us His presence. That means that He's always with us and helping us, especially when we're scared—just like when David had to fight off lions and bears to protect his sheep (1 Samuel 17:34–36). David must have been terrified! But he knew God would help him. Chances are, you aren't going to be fighting off bears or lions. But you might have to show your science project to the whole class, talk to a friend who hurt your feelings, or even stand up for what's right. Don't be afraid. Because whether it's time to fight or take flight, God will help you.

EXPLORE THE WONDER

Whenever you're afraid, check out Psalm 23. It reminds us that God is our Shepherd who gives us everything we need. He has a rod to fight off enemies, and His staff helps us know which way to go. God even prepares a feast for us. It's not a feast of food, though. It's a feast of all the blessings, wisdom, and strength we need. What else does God promise to give us in Psalm 23?

God, thank You that even when I am afraid, You are with me. I will trust You to fight my battles for me. Amen.

WHO GOES THERE?

[Christ] is your example, and you
must follow in his steps.

1 PETER 2:21 NLT

Animals are everywhere—including your own backyard, even if you live in the city! You may not see them, but if you know what to look for, you can see where they've been. How? By their tracks. Just as we leave footprints when we walk through snow, dirt, sand, or mud, animals leave tracks. Each animal has its own kind of track, and by knowing what to look for, you can figure out who's been there.

For example, animals in the dog family (like coyotes and foxes) have four toes on both their front and back feet, with little triangle shapes at the top of the toes where the claws are. Cats also have four toes on their front and back feet, but their claws don't show. Chipmunks, squirrels, and mice have four toes on their front feet, but five toes on their back. If you see five-toed tracks that look like little handprints, that's probably a raccoon. Two-toed prints are probably deer.

Just as you can identify an animal by its tracks, people can identify you by your tracks. Not the tracks you leave in the mud, but the tracks you leave in the world. And just as a puppy's tracks look like its family's tracks, your tracks should look like Jesus' tracks (John 13:35). That means you leave tracks like being kind to that kid no one else really talks to, being patient when you have to wait your turn, and helping out whenever you can. Most of all, it means doing everything with love—because those are the kinds of tracks Jesus leaves behind.

Lord, You leave tracks of love and kindness everywhere. Teach me to do the same everywhere I go. Amen.

EXPLORE THE WONDER

Grab a friend or parent, head outside, and get tracking! Check your backyard or neighborhood, search the playground, or head to a park. Live in the city? Look for cat footprints on windshields, shiny snail trails on the sidewalk, or the scratches from squirrels on trees. How many different animal prints can you find?

A MIGHTY BLOWING WIND

Suddenly a noise came from heaven. It
sounded like a strong wind blowing. . . .
They were all filled with the Holy Spirit.

ACTS 2:2, 4 ICB

El Niño means "the Christ child," and it's the name of a pattern of weather that happens in the Pacific Ocean about every two to 10 years. Scientists don't know when it will come, but when it does, El Niño sticks around for about nine to 12 months. It can even last 18 months—or

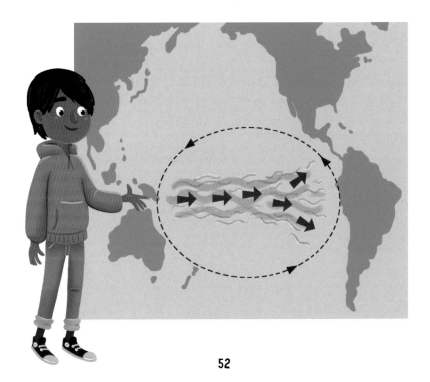

longer! Fishermen named it El Niño because it usually comes close to Christmas.

What does El Niño do? Well, in normal years, the waters near the equator are warmed by the Sun. Strong winds push those warm waters away from the coasts of South America and the United States, leaving cooler waters in their place. But in El Niño years, the winds blow *the other way*. They push warm waters into South America and up toward California. Fish that like cooler waters swim away, and tropical fish swim in to take their places. El Niño also brings lots more rain and clouds. And it all starts with a mighty blowing wind.

Acts 2:2 talks about something far more powerful than El Niño. The Holy Spirit "blew" into the disciples' lives and changed them forever. He brought the power of God to live inside them! The Spirit gave them courage when they were afraid, comfort when they were sad, and words when they didn't know what to say. But the Holy Spirit wasn't just for those long-ago disciples. When you choose to love and follow Jesus, the Holy Spirit will also blow into your life as powerful as a mighty wind.

Lord, fill me with Your Spirit. Come into my life, change me, and make me more like Jesus. Amen.

La Niña means "the little girl" in Spanish, and it's the opposite of El Niño. La Niña *cools* off the waters near South America and California. Places that get more rain during El Niño might have a drought during La Niña. And while El Niño causes more tropical storms in the Pacific, La Niña builds up stronger storms in the Atlantic Ocean.

UP, UP, AND AWAY!

Let us think about each other and help each
other to show love and do good deeds.

HEBREWS 10:24 ICB

Imagine a balloon so big that an entire football stadium could fit
inside! That's exactly the kind of balloon NASA uses. Not for birthday
parties, but for learning more about Earth and space.

Space balloons can lift up to 8,000 pounds—about as much as three
small cars! These balloons are made out of a thin plastic that's about as thick
as a sandwich bag. And they can soar as high as 26 miles into the sky. That's

not quite outer space. Scientists call it "near space," and there's only about 1 percent of Earth's atmosphere up there. That lets scientists do all kinds of experiments—like studying how space affects bacteria and viruses or testing out new equipment for future spacecrafts. It's a lot easier than sending a whole rocket into space! Just like party balloons, NASA's balloons are filled with helium gas. Helium is lighter than air, so it rises, lifting the balloons up into the sky.

You can be like one of those giant space balloons—not floating off toward space but lifting up those around you. Everyone has troubles, and those troubles can feel so heavy that they drag people down. But you can make a friend's troubles seem lighter with a smile, a kind word, or a hug. Listen to friends who need to talk, help if you can, and pray for those who are struggling. Fill them up with love and kindness—and always point them to God. He can lift anyone up, up, and away from trouble!

Lord, help me see the hurting people around me and do all I can to lift them up. Amen.

EXPLORE THE WONDER

If you lived back in the 1300s and wanted balloons for your birthday, you'd be playing with air-filled pig bladders. Gross! It wasn't until 1824 that Michael Faraday invented the first rubber balloon. He did it by pressing together the edges of two sheets of rubber. Do-it-yourself balloon kits appeared about a year after that. Finally, in 1847, J. G. Ingram invented the modern toy balloon—although they didn't start "popping" up at birthday parties until the 1930s!

WHEN YOU DON'T SAY A WORD

What good is it, dear brothers and
sisters, if you say you have faith but
don't show it by your actions?

JAMES 2:14 NLT

We move our lips to talk, right? Well, sometimes we do, and sometimes we don't. In fact, we can have a whole conversation without moving our lips or making a sound. Don't believe me? How many times have you and your best friend "talked" in class without the teacher hearing a thing?

Eye rolls, shoulder shrugs, head nods, eyebrow raises, and hand waves—we use these nonverbal movements to "say" things without saying a word. It's called body language. But it's more than just the movements we make on purpose. It's also the things we do without really thinking about it. Like the way we sit up straight when we're paying attention or slump down when we're bored. Or how our big eyes and wishful face say we really want that last cookie, even when we say we don't. Our bodies are always "talking," and they say a lot about what we're really feeling inside.

The same thing happens with our actions. We might say all the right things about loving Jesus and trying to be more like Him, but our actions speak a lot louder than our words. They show what we really think. That's why people believe what you *do* more than what you *say*. So don't just talk about loving Jesus. Show people what that love looks like by helping others, being kind, and praising Him. Because when your lips aren't moving, that's sometimes when you're "talking" the loudest.

Lord, I love You. Teach me how to show that to others in everything I do—when I'm speaking and when I'm not. Amen.

EXPLORE THE WONDER

A personal bubble has nothing to do with bubblegum. It's the space you like to have between yourself and others. Your bubble's size changes depending on who you're with (friend or stranger), where you are (home or store), and what you're doing (reading or playing a game). In America, most people like to stay about 1½ to 4 feet apart, but in Japan bubbles are only about 10 inches apart!

27

A FORTRESS TO GO

The LORD is my rock, my fortress
and my deliverer; my God is my
rock, in whom I take refuge.

PSALM 18:2 NIV

Imagine carrying your own personal fortress everywhere you go. Having a bad day? Duck inside. Bully headed your way? Time for the fortress. Forgot the big test? Uh-oh, time to hide! That's life for turtles. Well, except for the test part. From the 1,500-pound leatherback turtle to the tiny three-inch Cape tortoise, the one thing they all have in common is their shell.

That shell is made up of about 60 bones and covered with tough plates called scutes (skoots). The shell acts like a rib cage to protect the turtle's soft body. It's attached to their spine, so turtles can't climb out of their shell—no matter what you see in the cartoons! If threatened, turtles pull back into their shells. Some can only tuck their neck in sideways. Others can pull their legs, feet, and entire head completely inside their shells. Talk about a fortress!

There are days when that kind of protection would come in handy, right? But you might look a little silly carrying a big shell on your back. You do have your own personal fortress, though. It's even tougher than a turtle's shell—it's God! So if it's been a bad day or you find yourself in a tough spot, call on God. Ask Him to wrap you up in His love and give you the wisdom to know what to do. God is with you wherever you go, so go to Him as your fortress whenever you need protection!

Lord, there is nothing and no one stronger than You. Thank You for the fortress of Your love and protection. Amen.

EXPLORE THE WONDER

Turtles, tortoises, and terrapins. What's the difference? Well, they're all part of the reptile group called Testudines. Tortoises stay on land, though, while turtles spend most of their lives in water, only coming out to lay eggs or soak up the Sun. Terrapins are equally comfortable on land and in water. You'll find these tiptoeing creatures living around swamps, rivers, or ponds.

Leatherback sea turtle

28

ALL THE LiGHT

Wash me, and I will be whiter than snow.

PSALM 51:7 ICB

Catch a snowflake on your mitten, and it looks like a tiny crystal jewel. A *clear* crystal jewel. So why does snow on the ground—or rolled up into a snowman—look white?

First, let's look at that single snowflake. It's clear because it's made of ice crystals. As many as *200* ice crystals in just one snowflake! And since it takes about a bajillion snowflakes to make a pile of snow, imagine how many ice

crystals that is. At least a gazillion! When light hits all those crystals, they reflect it all back like so many shiny little mirrors.

Now, light is made up of all the different colors. When light hits most objects, some colors are absorbed, or soaked up. Others are reflected back. For example, a yellow flower soaks up all the light *except* yellow, so you see yellow. Snow doesn't absorb any colors. It reflects them *all* back. And when all the colors of light are added together, they look white. That's why snow looks white.

We should be like snow. I don't mean cold and icy—I mean we should reflect back *all* the light. You see, God shines the light of His love into our lives. When we try to love others the way He loves us—to be kind, gentle, patient, and forgiving—we reflect that light. The more we love, the more light we reflect. So let's be like snow! How can you reflect God's light into the world today?

God, it's hard to even understand how much You love me, but I'm so thankful You do. Help me to shine by loving others the way You love me. Amen.

Watermelon snow in Alaska

Snow isn't *always* white. When large amounts of snow get packed together, it can have a blueish color instead. (Use a stick to poke a hole in a snowbank, and you might see that faint blue color.) Snow can even be pink or red! That's called watermelon snow, and it's usually found high in the mountains. The color comes from red algae. So even though it looks like candy, it's definitely not tasty!

29

A NEW WAY TO SHINE!

Sing to the Lord a new song. Sing
to the Lord, all the earth.

PSALM 96:1 ICB

There's a new comet in town. Well, it's not really new, but it's newly discovered. It's NEOWISE (NEE-oh-wahyz), and it's named after the *NEOWISE* spacecraft that first spotted it on March 27, 2020. (*NEOWISE* stands for Near-Earth Object Wide-field Infrared Survey Explorer.)

What's a comet? It's a huge chunk of ice, dust, and rock that orbits—or circles—the Sun. Comets are often several miles across, and many are about the size of a small town. As a comet gets close to the Sun, the ice and dust start to vaporize—or burn up—from the heat. This forms a glowing tail that can stretch for thousands or even millions of miles!

The NEOWISE comet came closest to Earth in July 2020, when it was "only" about 64 million miles away. Both the Hubble Telescope and the International Space Station snapped a picture as it zoomed by. NEOWISE is now rocketing away from us at about 144,000 miles per hour. It won't come close to Earth again for another 7,000 years!

For a little while, NEOWISE was a brand-new bright spot shining in the solar system. So why not let it inspire you to find a new way to shine? Write a song, paint a picture, run a race, lead a prayer, or volunteer. Explore the universe of talents God has given you and use them to honor and praise Him. Because when you do, you—and the world around you—shine brighter than ever before!

God, sometimes trying new things can be a little scary. Help me be brave enough to do things that help me grow and bring You glory. Amen.

EXPLORE THE WONDER

From 2009 until 2011, the *WISE* spacecraft scanned space for asteroids, stars, and other galaxies. Then it went *dormant*—which means it kind of went to sleep. NASA woke it up in 2013, changed its name to *NEOWISE*, and told it to hunt for asteroids and comets in our solar system. Since then, it's found more than 38,000 objects in our solar system, including over 200 comets!

30

DON'T JUST COMPLAIN ABOUT IT

I pour out my complaints before him
and tell him all my troubles.

PSALM 142:2 NLT

Why do I have to wait? I don't wanna be a tree in the play. I don't like this game. Everybody complains. In fact, researchers have figured out that when we're talking to someone, we complain about once every 60 seconds. But that's not the worst part: complaining actually changes the brain and makes us complain even more!

The brain likes to build little shortcuts for the things it does most often. So if you complain a lot, your brain's neurons (NYOOR-ons) arrange themselves to make that easier to do. (Neurons are cells that carry messages

through the brain.) The trouble is, those shortcuts make it harder to do other things, like be grateful. Researchers also found that just listening to someone else complain causes your neurons to start moving around. Now, that's something to complain about!

Yes, there are times to complain, like when a problem needs fixing. For example, if the restaurant forgot to put cheese on your cheeseburger. But there's a right way to complain. Go to the person who can fix the problem. Say, "Excuse me . . ." and politely explain what's wrong. When they fix it, smile and say thank you. (If they don't fix it, you might need to get a grown-up to help.)

Don't complain just to complain. If there's a real problem, go to the one who can fix it. When it's the cheese for your cheeseburger, that's the person at the restaurant. For bigger things in life, that's God. He's the One who can fix your troubles, so talk to Him. Then trust Him to do what's best—and quit complaining.

Lord, when things aren't going my way, remind me to go to the One who can fix it instead of constantly complaining. Amen.

People have been complaining for a very, very, *very* long time. And sometimes they put it in writing. Archaeologists (people who dig up and study the stuff from the past) found a 4,000-year-old tablet from ancient Mesopotamia. It was a complaint from a customer. He wasn't happy with the pieces of copper he bought and wanted his money back!

65

WHATEVER YOU NEED

My God will use his wonderful riches in Christ
Jesus to give you everything you need.

PHILIPPIANS 4:19 ICB

Pandas might look like super-cute, somersaulting teddy bears, but they're called *giant* pandas for a reason. Male pandas weigh up to 250 pounds—that's more than three 10-year-old kids! Female pandas are slightly less giant at about 200 pounds.

To grow into their giant size, pandas eat bamboo—lots of it! So it's probably a good thing they live in China's bamboo forests. Bamboo isn't the easiest or healthiest food to eat, though. It's tough and doesn't have much nutritional value. To stay full and healthy, pandas need to eat more than 30 pounds of bamboo every day. They spend around 12 hours a day just eating! To help with all that chowing down, pandas have an extra finger on their paws. It works like a thumb to help hold the bamboo. They also have broad, flat teeth to crush the tough stalks.

From bamboo forests to thumbs and special teeth, God gives the giant panda everything it needs to be the panda He created it to be. And you know what? He does the same thing for you and me. God makes sure you have everything you need to be the person He created you to be and to do everything He created you to do. He'll give you courage when you're scared, wisdom when you're not sure what to do, joy when you're sad, and so much love. God's got an unlimited supply of whatever you need!

God, thank You for giving me everything I need to live, to love, and to be who You created me to be. Amen.

EXPLORE THE WONDER

Did you know red pandas tweet? It's probably not the kind of tweet you're thinking of—they don't get online much. Their tweet is a kind of twittering "talk" that sounds more like a bird than a bear. Of course, that could be because red pandas aren't bears. Instead, they're more closely related to raccoons and skunks. Red pandas also squeal, hiss, and grunt—when they're not tweeting, that is!

A LiTTLE HELP, PLEASE

Help each other with your troubles.

GALATIANS 6:2 ICB

Imagine getting a text message from Antarctica every two hours. That's exactly what happens for scientists at the National Institute of Water and Atmospheric Research in New Zealand. Well, actually, they get a text from instruments under the Antarctic ice shelf.

An ice shelf is a gigantic slab of floating ice, and about 300 of them are around the coast of Antarctica. Some of them are shrinking, and scientists want to know why. But the waters around the Antarctic are frozen most of the year, and getting there isn't always possible. So scientists figured out some amazing ways to get the information they need. Satellites in space measure how thick the ice is. Robotic submarines travel under the ice shelves to map them and chart any changes. Even animals get in on the action! A group called Marine Mammals Exploring the Oceans Pole to Pole (MEOP) uses special electronic tags attached to seals, penguins, and other marine animals to gather information from places humans can't go.

The scientists couldn't get the information on their own, so they let others—creatures and machines—help them. That's a good thing, and not just for scientists. Because no one can do everything. Whether it's learning to dribble a soccer ball, reaching something on the top shelf, or figuring out what a Bible verse means, we all need help sometimes. Don't be too proud to ask for it. And be sure to ask God too, because He's always there to help you.

Speaking of ice, scientists drilled a hole through the Antarctic ice shelf. They were hoping to check out the ocean floor underneath, but what they found was life! A whole little community of sponges and other unknown stationary animals. (*Stationary* means they can't move.) Until this discovery, no one believed these kinds of animals could live in the dark, freezing-cold waters under the ice shelf. How cool is that?

God, it's hard to admit I need help sometimes. Forgive me for being too proud and help me learn that it's okay to ask for help—especially from You. Amen.

gamma rays

IN A BURST OF LIGHT

With your wisdom and power you created
the earth and spread out the heavens.

JEREMIAH 10:12 CEV

G amma rays—they're the stuff of science fiction and comic books. Or are they? Turns out gamma rays are *real*. They're a kind of light. You see, there are different kinds of light, but it's all energy that travels in waves. The light we see travels in medium-length waves. Microwaves—like the ones that pop our popcorn—are longer. X-rays travel in shorter waves, and gamma rays are the shortest of all.

The shorter the wave, the more energy it has. So gamma rays have *a lot* of energy—about a billion times more energy than the light we see. On Earth, nuclear explosions and lightning can create gamma rays. In space, gamma rays are caused by big events like a star explosion. Gamma rays are so powerful that you'd need a concrete shield over 6½ feet thick to protect you from all the energy.

Since gamma rays are so powerful, just imagine how powerful the God who made them must be. *Nothing* is impossible for Him! He can build planets, stretch out the skies, and create light and energy with one breath. His power is absolutely endless—and so is His love for you. Yes, God is more powerful than you could ever understand. But He is never too big or too busy to listen to you. Tell Him your hopes, dreams, worries, troubles, and fears. And then watch as He starts pouring His power into helping you.

God, You have such a large world and universe to take care of. Thank You for always taking time to listen to me. Amen.

EXPLORE THE WONDER

In January 2019, the Hubble Space Telescope captured something amazing: a gamma ray burst, or GRB. It was the most powerful burst ever seen. In a few seconds, that GRB gave off more energy than our Sun will in its entire life! The burst came from a galaxy five billion light-years away. Scientists think it may have been caused by a dying star.

Hubble Space Telescope

ONE FACE OR TWO?

You are God's children whom he
loves, so try to be like him.

EPHESIANS 5:1 NCV

Do you see her? Just take a look at this picture of a beautiful, young woman. I mean old woman. No, I mean . . . which is it? Actually, it's both! Can you see the young woman *and* the old? (Try looking for the young woman's chin. Then, picture that chin as the old woman's nose.) This picture is an example of an optical illusion (OP-ti-kuhl ih-LOO-zhuhn).

Optical illusions happen when our brains get confused about what our eyes are seeing. Our eyes' job is to take in the information they see—like the size, shape, and color of a dog running toward us. But our brain tells us what we're seeing and says, "Hey, that's a dog running toward us!"

Optical illusions use light, color, and pattern to trick our brains. And they are kind of fun when it comes to pictures. But they're not so fun when it comes to people. Like when some kid pretends to be nice in front of the teacher. But when the teacher isn't looking, she cheats on a test or makes fun of the teacher. We call that being two-faced. Jesus called people like that hypocrites (HIP-uh-krits), and He said, "their hearts are far from me" (Matthew 15:8 ICB)—so it's definitely not a good thing to be. Instead, always try to be kind and good. Do what's right, even if no one is looking. That's the best way to be—and that's no illusion.

God, I don't want to pretend to be someone I'm not. Please give me the courage to be "real" and always do what's right, no matter who I am with. Amen.

One of the most beautiful optical illusions was created by God Himself: Antelope Canyon in Arizona. Over the years, water washed away bits of the rock, creating tall, wavy "slots" in the canyon's walls. When the Sun rises, light darts in and out of those slots—making it look like the whole canyon is on fire!

Check out this optical illusion! How many legs does the elephant have?

73

HOW RUDE!

Make it your goal to live a quiet life,
minding your own business.
1 THESSALONIANS 4:11 NLT

White rhinos are one of the biggest land mammals in the entire world. In fact, they're tied with hippos as the second biggest—only the elephant is bigger. In spite of their huge size, rhinos have a little secret: they eavesdrop. Or at least the male rhinos do. Eavesdropping means listening in on people's—er, rhinos'—conversations. Rhinos do it to protect their territory. If a male rhino hears another male "talking," he'll eavesdrop to see if that other rhino is just passing through or trying to take over his territory.

By listening, the rhino can also tell if the other rhino is younger or older. If it's younger, he'll probably head on over and chase it away. But if it's older—and probably more experienced at fighting—the rhino takes his time, eavesdropping a little longer to make sure it's a fight he can win.

Rhinos have a good reason to eavesdrop, but we almost never do. (Unless you're a super-secret-agent spy. But then you're too busy saving the world to read this book!) Eavesdropping is rude, and it can cause trouble. You might ruin a surprise. You might misunderstand, like getting upset because your parents are talking about moving when they just want to move the couch. Or you might hear a hurtful secret that someone isn't ready to share. So the next time you start to hear someone else's conversation, be wise—mind your own business and point your ears in another direction.

Lord, it's so tempting to listen to other people's private conversations. Help me choose to mind my own business and focus on listening to You instead. Amen.

EXPLORE THE WONDER

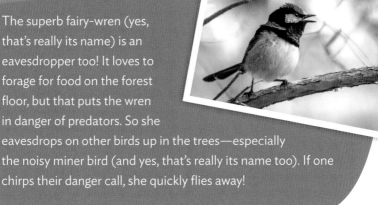

The superb fairy-wren (yes, that's really its name) is an eavesdropper too! It loves to forage for food on the forest floor, but that puts the wren in danger of predators. So she eavesdrops on other birds up in the trees—especially the noisy miner bird (and yes, that's really its name too). If one chirps their danger call, she quickly flies away!

FiGHTiNG FiRE
WiTH . . . FiRE?

A gentle answer will calm a person's anger.
But an unkind answer will cause more anger.

PROVERBS 15:1 ICB

To put out a fire, you would need water or a fire extinguisher, right? What about more fire? It sounds crazy, but firefighters sometimes use fire to fight fires. Especially when they're fighting wildfires.

A wildfire is a fire that's burning out of control, often in a forest. In the US, wildfires can pop up anywhere, but the biggest ones happen in the west in places like California, Nevada, and Oregon. Those areas have a rainy season which encourages trees, shrubs, and grasses to grow. That's followed by a long, hot, dry season. All those trees and grasses get so dry that a single spark—from a firecracker or a bolt of lightning—can set off a huge fire!

To fight wildfires, firefighters try to get rid of the plants and trees the fire "eats." In a ring of dirt around the fire, they pull out all the plants, creating a firebreak, where the fire stops spreading. Or they might start a backfire—that's a small fire set in front of the big fire. Backfires gobble up the smaller plants and dead wood. With nothing left to burn, the wildfire "starves" and dies out.

EXPLORE THE WONDER

Fight fire with drones? Yep! Because they're small, drones can fly into places that helicopters and airplanes can't go. They can map out how big a fire is, which way it's moving, and how fast. They can even drop Dragon Eggs, which are Ping Pong–sized balls that explode when they hit the ground to set small backfires.

Fighting fire with fire works great for wildfires. But it's a terrible idea when it comes to any other kind of fire—especially fire with other people. If someone says something insulting or mean, it's tempting to fight fire with fire and say something mean right back. But that only creates a bigger fire. Try sharing a kind word instead. When you take away their reason to "burn" with anger, their fire will soon die out.

God, it's so easy to answer mean words with even more mean words. Help me have self-control and say something kind instead. Amen.

UNDER PRESSURE!

I was in trouble. So I called to the Lord.
The Lord answered me and set me free.

PSALM 118:5 ICB

There's a moon out tonight. Oh, wait. There are two moons. No, 79! If you happen to live on Jupiter, that is. And actually, there might be more than 79—that's just how many astronomers have found so far.

Io (EYE-oh) is one of those moons, but it's nothing like Earth's peaceful, nighttime friend. Over 400 active volcanoes cover Io's surface, and they are constantly erupting, shooting fountains of lava over 200 miles high! Io is over

390 million miles away, but its explosions are so powerful that they can sometimes be seen from Earth (using an extra-huge telescope, of course!). Io also has *a ton* of lightning and lakes of molten lava.

Why is Io so explosive? The gravity from Jupiter and other nearby moons pushes and pulls on the moon, which makes the land move. *A lot.* Just trying to stand on Io would be like riding a roller coaster! All that movement builds up pressure and heat until the material inside Io gets so hot that it melts, boils, then, boom . . . it blows!

The same thing can happen to us. Not the spewing lava part. But we all face lots of pressures. The pressure to fit in, to earn a good grade, to never mess up. *So much pressure!* It all comes down to the pressure to be perfect—and nobody is perfect. But all that pressure can make you heat up inside. When you feel like you're going to blow up in an angry outburst, get up and get moving. Burn off some of that pressure with exercise. And while you're moving, talk to God. He already knows what's going on, and He can set you free from all that pressure.

Lord, when the pressure to be perfect makes me want to blow up in anger or stress, help me remember that You are in control and I am perfectly loved by You. Amen.

SHARE THE WONDER

The pressure to be perfect hits pretty much everybody. Take some of that pressure away before there's an explosion. The next time you see someone feeling that pressure to be perfect, remind them of how awesome they already are. Point out the things they're great at. And tell them God loves them, no matter what—and that you do too!

BRRR! BRAIN FREEZE

"At that time the Holy Spirit will
teach you what you must say."

LUKE 12:12 ICB

You're slurping up your favorite slushie (mine's cherry) when suddenly there's this stabbing pain right behind your eyeballs. Ouch! What's happening? Don't worry. It's just a little *sphenopalatine ganglioneuralgia*. Let's skip figuring out how to say *that* and just call this splitting headache by its everyday name: brain freeze.

Scientists can't completely explain brain freeze. But they do know what causes it: quickly eating cold foods or slurping down cold drinks, like giant cherry slushies. Scientists believe the cold food cools the palate (PAL-it), or roof of your mouth, and changes the blood flow to the brain. That triggers nearby nerves to say "Ouch!" and then you've got a headache. Scientists think it might be the body's way of protecting the brain from getting too cold—or "freezing." That's why we call it brain freeze. And because it's much easier to say than *sphenopalatine ganglioneuralgia*.

There's another kind of brain freeze too. It happens when we suddenly can't think of what to say. It usually happens when we're nervous, like in front of a big crowd, or when we're trying to tell someone about Jesus. Perhaps that's because we think talking about Jesus is so important that we don't want to mess it up, or we're afraid the other person will reject us. To stop brain freeze, "warm up" by thinking about what you want to say ahead of time, practice saying it, and, most important of all, pray. Because God promises that His Holy Spirit will help you know what to say. And trust me, it'll be a lot easier to say than *sphenopalatine ganglioneuralgia*!

God, sometimes I'm afraid I'll say the wrong thing. Please help me know what to say and confidently tell others about You. Amen.

EXPLORE THE WONDER

Got a case of brain freeze that you want to fix fast? Push your tongue up against the roof of your mouth. (Or you can use your thumb—just make sure it's clean!) The warmth will calm down those blood vessels and nerves and ease the pain. And next time, slurp up that slushie a little slower.

NATURE'S CLEAN-UP CREW

The LORD God took the man and put him in the
Garden of Eden to work it and take care of it.

GENESIS 2:15 NIV

Coyotes, vultures, cockroaches, and sharks—meet the *scavengers!* These animals eat trash, rotting plants, and carrion (KER-ee-uhn), which is the scientific word for dead animals. *Yuck!* Just think, though. What if that stuff never got cleaned up? What a huge, dangerous mess that would be! Because all of that rotting stuff is the perfect place for diseases and harmful bacteria to grow.

That's where scavengers come in. These animals are specially designed to take care of the trash. Like vultures—their bald heads are easier to keep clean, and super-strong stomach acid means they can eat even rotten meat without getting sick.

You'll find scavengers just about everywhere. Vultures and ravens fly through the skies, looking for dead things to eat. Insects like cockroaches and flies help too. Mammals, such as coyotes, foxes, and even polar bears, do their part. Turtles help keep rivers tidy. Crabs, lobsters, and sharks are on the job in the seas.

Isn't it wonderful how God takes care of our world? He even created animals to take care of the trash! You can be part of God's clean-up crew too! Start with the world right around you. Make it a habit to walk around your neighborhood or street once a week and pick up any trash you see. Be sure to wear gloves, and let a grown-up handle dangerous stuff, like broken glass. If we each take care of our corner of the world, we can keep this planet God gave us clean!

Lord, thank You for this amazing world You've given us. Open my eyes to see how I can be part of Your clean-up crew. Amen.

EXPLORE THE WONDER

Have you ever noticed a bunch of butterflies on a patch of mud? What are they doing? Scavenging! That's right, those dainty little creatures are scavengers too. Butterflies gather on patches of mud, dung, or even dead animals and fish—and lick up the salts and other minerals they can't get from flowers. It's called mud-puddling!

40

THE WONDER INSIDE

God has made everything
beautiful for its own time.

ECCLESIASTES 3:11 NLT

Not every rock is just a rock. Some have a crystal treasure hidden inside. They're called geodes (JEE-ohdz). *Geode* comes from the Greek word *geodes* meaning "earthlike." After all, geodes are usually round. Most are about the size of a tennis ball. But some are as small as a dime, while others are as big as your bedroom—or even bigger!

Geodes are created in the empty spaces inside tree roots, old animal burrows, or even rocks. The tree roots rot away, and of course, animals dig out burrows, leaving empty spaces. But how does an empty space form inside a rock? It can happen when lava bubbles up from volcanoes. Those bubbles pop as the lava cools and turns to rock—leaving a hollow space. Water seeps into those spaces and leaves behind minerals, like quartz (kwawrts) or amethyst (AM-uh-thist). Over hundreds, even thousands of years, the minerals build up into beautiful crystals.

The largest known geode is so big you can walk right inside! Workers digging a well discovered it in 1897. They first thought it was a cave, but it was actually one single rock—a geode. The walls were—and still are—covered in celestite (SEL-uh-stahyt) crystals as long as three feet! It's called the Crystal Cave, and you can visit it in Put-in-Bay, Ohio.

God loves to surprise us with beauty—even inside a rock! Sometimes it's out in the open and easy to spot. But other times, He hides it like a treasure for us to find. For example, have you ever seen a broken seashell? The inside is a swirl of color. Or how about the inside of a tree branch with all its rings? God tucks something wonderful into every part of His creation, and He's just waiting for you to discover it. Search for God's hidden wonders. And when you find one, praise the God who makes even the ordinary extraordinary!

God, thank You for the wonders all around me. Show me something today that I've never noticed before. Amen.

41

ROBOT ASTRONAUT

I will sing for joy about what your hands have
done. Lord, you have done such great things!

PSALM 92:4–5 ICB

You've heard of astronauts, but have you heard of Robonaut?
He's a robot astronaut. And he's part of the crew on board the
International Space Station, which was first launched into space in 1998.

When Robonaut first arrived at the Space Station in 2011, he was just a
body, arms, and a head. Kind of creepy, huh? But after a "quick" trip back to
Earth in 2014, Robonaut now has legs. Instead of feet, he has clamps for holding on. Robonaut is learning to do simple jobs around the Space Station, like
changing air filters and cleaning up.

Why send robots into space? They can go dangerous places humans can't go, like where temperatures are too hot or cold. They don't need oxygen, food, or water. They don't have to sleep, and they can survive for years in space. NASA is now working on Robonauts that will one day serve as explorers and scouts to places like Mars.

Robonaut—or R2 as his friends call him—is pretty amazing. I mean, he's a robot! In space! But even though scientists have created one cool robot, he's nothing compared to God's creation: us. Even Robonaut's fancy new, multi-million dollar legs are just a clunky imitation of our own legs. Sure, R2 can hold on to things. But we can walk, run, roller-skate, and dance. God made each of us in a marvelous and wonderful way (Psalm 139:14). So while robots might look all cool, it's God's creation—you—that's the coolest!

God, I praise You for the wonderful way You have made me. Thank You for making me more amazing than any robot could ever be. Amen.

EXPLORE THE WONDER

NASA has a lot more robots in the works! There's PUFFER, or Pop-Up Flat Folding Explorer Rover. This two-wheeled robot can flatten itself out to explore small, tight spaces. (The idea came from origami!) Cube-shaped Hedgehog is built to hop and tumble across asteroids and comets. And then there's Valkyrie—a more human-shaped robot—that's being built for future settlements on Mars!

Hedgehog, the hopping and tumbling robot

42

TO CURL OR NOT TO CURL?

The Lord's eyes see everything that happens.

PROVERBS 15:3 ICB

To curl or not to curl? That is the question. Well, actually the question is, *Why do some people have curly hair and others have straight?* The answer is all in the follicles (FOL-i-kuhls). Follicles are tiny organs, like your

heart and lungs, except much, much smaller! They sit just inside your scalp, and their job is to make new hair. Once a follicle creates the new hair, it pushes it up through a tube and out of your scalp. The shape of the follicle decides if you'll have straight hair or curly. A round follicle will create straight hair, while an oval follicle can give hair just a little wave or a twisty-tight curl.

Straight or curly, God knows every hair on your head (Matthew 10:30). That's because God *sees* you—and not just the way you look. He sees your thoughts, feelings, worries, and fears. That's not because He's super-nosy. It's because He loves you. And because God sees and knows everything about you, He knows exactly how to help you. God wants you to see people too. Not just the way they look or what they're doing,

Your hair is golden, no matter what color it is. That's because your hair contains microscopic bits of gold—about two milligrams worth. Yeah, it's not a lot—a single paperclip weighs about 1,000 milligrams. How did it get there? You ate it! There's gold in the Earth's water and soil. Plants soak up that gold, animals eat the plants, and we eat both! Talk about "goldilocks"!

but *how* they're doing. Pay attention. Does your mom need a hug? Does your dad need to laugh over a goofy joke? Does a friend need to talk? What do you see? And what can you do about what you see? Don't just keep walking straight on by. Give a wave, curl an arm around a friend—let people know that you see them.

Lord, teach me to really see the people around me. And help me do what I can do to help them and show them Your love. Amen.

JUST LET IT ROLL

Even before he made the world, God loved
us and chose us in Christ to be holy.

EPHESIANS 1:4 NLT

Ducks are called *waterfowl,* and you'll never guess why! It's because they are fowl (which is another name for birds) and because they live near the water. Get it? Okay, yeah, you probably figured that one out for yourself.

Because ducks spend most of their lives in water, they need a way to stay warm and dry. That's why God gave them feathers—actually, two different kinds of feathers. Down is made of soft, fluffy feathers close to their skin. Down feathers trap pockets of air that act like insulation to keep the ducks warm. On top of the down is a set of larger, stiffer feathers. Each one has little hooked barbicels (BAR-bih-sels) along the edges that zip together like Velcro. They create a watertight seal and keep the ducks dry—even if they dive underwater. Once they pop up to the surface again, the water just rolls right off.

That's what we should do too—not the part about the water but letting things roll off. Insults and mean words can stab your heart just like a sword. But—and this is important—they lose their power to hurt you when you remember what God says about you: you are chosen by Him! Let the truth of how much He loves you wrap around you like soft feathers and keep you warm. And let the fact that you are *His* wonderfully made child cover you like a waterproof seal—and those mean words will just roll off like water off a duck's back.

God, when someone hurts my feelings with their words, help me remember who I really am—Your child! Amen.

SHARE THE WONDER

People need to hear good things about themselves. In fact, scientists say it takes at least five good comments to make up for just one mean comment. Since you never know who is having a bad day, try to say something positive to everyone you meet. But don't just use any ol' words. Make sure what you say is helpful, kind, and true. Challenge yourself to encourage someone every day!

THAT'S NO JOKE!

Careless words stab like a sword.
But wise words bring healing.

PROVERBS 12:18 ICB

Yellowstone National Park sits right on top of an active volcano! That means a lot of magma (or melted rock) is stirring around under the ground. In some places, that magma heats up the underground water and forms geysers (GAHY-serz). The water can get so hot that it erupts, spewing water and steam high into the air.

Old Faithful is the most famous geyser. Can you guess why it's called Old Faithful? Because it faithfully erupts about 20 times a day. Every one to two

hours, Old Faithful sends thousands of gallons of water and steam shooting 100 to 180 feet high in the sky! Each eruption lasts from a minute and a half to five minutes. And that water is hot—about 204 degrees Fahrenheit. (Water boils at 212 degrees!) The steam is even hotter at 350 degrees. So don't get too close! All that spewing water and steam can cause a terrible burn!

Geysers aren't the only things that can spew and cause burns. Our words can do the same thing. Some people think it's funny to "burn" others with insults. They might even say, "I'm just kidding" or "It's just a joke!" But *burn* is the perfect way to describe the pain these kinds of words cause. Here's a tip: if you say, "I'm joking," then that's no joke. Make sure you're laughing *with* someone and not *at* them. Be caring—not careless—with your words. If you want to make someone laugh, tell a real joke instead. Like this one: *Knock knock.* Who's there? *Hatch.* Hatch who? *God bless you!*

God, I'm sorry for the times I've "burned" people with my words. Help me use my words to make people smile instead. Amen.

Handkerchief Pool in the Yellowstone National Park

Have a dirty handkerchief? Well, if you happened to be in Yellowstone about a hundred years ago, you could just toss it into the Handkerchief Pool. After a minute, it would get sucked down into the pool—only to pop up again much cleaner! Sadly, too many people threw too much junk into the pool and clogged it up. You can still visit the pool. Just keep your handkerchief in your pocket.

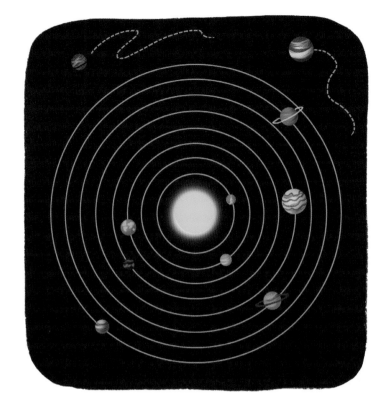

GO YOUR OWN WAY

"Those who know my commands and
obey them are the ones who love me."

JOHN 14:21 NCV

The planets of our solar system—Mercury, Venus, Earth, Mars, Jupiter, Saturn, Uranus, and Neptune, and even dwarf planet Pluto—all *orbit*, or circle, around the Sun. Each planet has its own path as it circles around and around. But that's not true for every planet in the universe. Starting in the 1990s, astronomers discovered rogue planets. *Rogue* (ROHG) means something doesn't act the way it is expected to act. These planets don't act like astronomers expect them to. That is, they don't orbit around a star, like Earth orbits around our Sun. Rogue planets just sort of drift through the universe, each one going its own way.

Astronomers think there are billions, trillions, even bazillions of rogue planets. Okay, that last one isn't a real number. But astronomers do believe there might be more rogue planets than there are stars.

Sometimes being a *rogue person* can be a very good thing. You see, in this world, so many people choose to do wrong that it's almost like we're expected to do wrong too—to lie, cheat, gossip, and steal. But God wants His people to be different. He calls it being "set apart" and "holy." It doesn't mean we're perfect or better than anyone else. It simply means we're trying to do the things that please Him. We're trying to live in a way that shows others how good He is. And in this world, that can be a pretty "rogue" thing to do!

God, sometimes it's hard to not go along with everyone else. Show me when I should go rogue and follow You—and then help me be brave enough to do it! Amen.

SHARE THE WONDER

Going your own way—even when it's God's way—can be a little lonely, and even a little scary. That's why we "rogues" need to stick together. When you see someone else standing up for what's right, join in and be a rogue too! And remember, whenever two or more people stick together and stand up for God, Jesus stands with you (Matthew 18:20)!

ARE YOU BLUSHING?

"My power works best in weakness."

2 CORINTHIANS 12:9 NLT

Imagine this: **You're walking down the hall and turn to wave at a friend.** As you turn back around, you walk—*SMACK!*—straight into a locker. As you look around to see if anyone noticed, your face suddenly feels hot, your heart is pounding, and your cheeks turn bright red. You're *blushing*!

Humans are the only animals that blush. Not dogs, horses, cats, or wombats. It happens when we're embarrassed. Or when we get caught doing something wrong. Like when the teacher calls on you, but you weren't really paying attention. It can even happen when someone is telling you how awesome you are. Being embarrassed can make you want to hide. But your face has suddenly turned into a glowing, bright red billboard telling the whole world how you feel.

Blushing happens when your emotions cause a reaction in your body. A hormone (HOR-mohn)—that's a chemical your body makes—called adrenaline (uh-DREN-uh-lin) is released. It causes tiny blood vessels called capillaries (KA-puh-ler-eez) to widen and carry more blood to your skin, which is why your face turns pink or red. You can't stop a blush from happening, but you can choose what you do next.

Shake it off. Laugh it off. Put it behind you. (Everybody walks into a locker or falls on their face now and then. Right?) Don't stay stuck in that moment, just thinking about it over and over again. Because no matter how many embarrassing mistakes you make, God is still working in your life. Let that truth make you strong! Not only is God working, but He also has wonderful plans for you.

Animals don't blush, but some of them laugh. Chimpanzees laugh when tickled or playing. Rats "chirp" when they're tickled. And dogs make a sort of laughing-panting sound when they're happy. Now, if you'll excuse me, I've got a great joke to share with my dog, London!

Lord, being embarrassed feels awful. But please help me to move on and not miss a moment with You. Amen.

97

SUMMER SNOOZiNG

[Jesus] said to them, "Come with me.
We will go to a quiet place to be alone.
There we will get some rest."

MARK 6:31 ICB

You've heard all about hibernation. That's when animals sleep through the winter. But some animals sleep through the summer instead. It's called estivation (eh-stuh-VAY-shun), or summer sleep. Bees, snails, ladybugs, frogs, crocodiles, and tortoises are just some of the animals that do their snoozing in the summertime. This usually happens in desert or tropical areas where temperatures are hot and food and water are hard to find. Animals find a spot that's cool, safe, and shady—like in a rotting tree or burrowed in the dirt or mud. Unlike winter sleepers, summer sleepers can wake easily if danger threatens or their environment changes. But until then, they take a break.

We don't take many breaks in our busy, busy world. So we could probably learn a thing or two from these summer snoozers. If you're like me, you have a lot that keeps you busy. Maybe for you it's practices, games, or recitals. Or homework, church, or chores. But everyone needs a break. That's why Jesus told His disciples to rest.

Rest doesn't have to mean sleep, though. Rest might also be doing something you enjoy, like playing outside, painting a picture, reading a book, or just curling up and hanging out with God for a while. When your life is busy with too much to do, remember what those summer sleepers do and take a break!

God, it's hard for me to rest—there always seems to be so much to do. Help me slow down and choose to simply be still with You. Amen.

EXPLORE THE WONDER

Kids spend about four to six hours a day with some sort of phone, TV, tablet, or computer screen. Sometimes it's more than one screen at a time! Too much screen time can cause sleep problems, weight gain, and lower grades. And it can really hurt your IRL (that's *in real life*) relationships. Take a break from the screens. Fly a kite, read a book, draw a picture, roll down a hill—do something IRL!

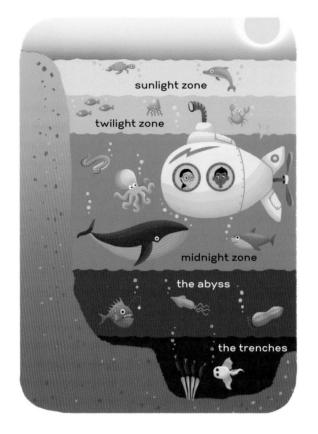

sunlight zone

twilight zone

midnight zone

the abyss

the trenches

48

WELCOME TO THE TWILIGHT ZONE

The sea is his because he made it.

PSALM 95:5 ICB

Did you know that it snows *in* the oceans? It's marine (muh-REEN) snow. (*Marine* means something connected to the sea.) You definitely don't want to make a snowman out of this stuff. Instead of ice crystals, this snow is made up of bits of dead plankton, dead animals, bacteria, and fecal (FEE-kuhl) pellets—also known as poop.

Don't worry, though. If you visit the ocean, you won't be swimming through this blizzard either. This snow is found in the twilight zone. That's the layer of water that lies between 650 and 3,300 feet below the surface. It's called the twilight zone because so little sunlight reaches it.

These waters are cold and dim, yet full of life. There are bacteria and teeny-tiny animals called zooplankton, along with fish, squid, and gelatinous (juh-LAT-in-uhs) animals (think living Jell-O). Marine snow may sound disgusting to us, but for these animals it's a tasty buffet. As they munch, they also clean up the oceans. And you can give them a hand. Er, tentacle . . . fin . . . oh, you know what I mean. One of the easiest and most helpful things you can do is to keep plastic out of the ocean by using less of it. Give reusable straws and water bottles a try. Use cloth bags instead of plastic. Reuse and recycle whenever you can. The oceans belong to God. And one way we can show our love for Him is to take care of them.

God, You created this world in amazing ways—even making animals to help keep it clean! Help me see all the ways I can work to clean it up too. Amen.

Scientists see the ocean as more than just a mass of water. They see it in layers. Kind of like a gigantic wet cake that's *really* salty. The top layer is known as the sunlight zone. Next comes the twilight zone, then the midnight zone. Below that is the abyss. And at the very bottom are the trenches. The bottom layer is 19,686 feet below the surface—that's over 3½ miles!

49

WHAT'S OORT THERE?

We are surrounded by a great cloud of
people whose lives tell us what faith means.

HEBREWS 12:1 NCV

If you could jump in a spacecraft and fly out past the Moon, past Neptune and Pluto, you'd find yourself in the Oort Cloud. The Oort (OR-t) Cloud surrounds our solar system like a humongous bubble. It's made up of billions of icy bits and space debris. Some are mountain-sized—or even bigger! This is where astronomers believe most comets come from.

The Oort Cloud is so far away that the *Voyager 1* spacecraft won't reach its edge for another 300 years—even though it left Earth in 1977 and is traveling about a million miles a day! After that, it will take *Voyager 1* another 30,000 years to travel all the way through the thick, thick cloud!

Just as the Oort Cloud surrounds our solar system, we are surrounded. Not by icy objects but by "a great cloud of people." They're the people who show us what it means to follow God. They can be parents, teachers, pastors, and friends. They can be modern-day faith heroes like Dietrich Bonhoeffer, who stood up to the Nazis in World War II Germany, or Elisabeth Elliot, who in 1958 became a missionary to the tribe that killed her husband. And they can be the people of the Bible, like Esther and Daniel, who teach us to be brave even when the whole world seems to be against us.

Living a life of faith isn't easy, but you're never alone. There's a great cloud of people to help and cheer you on!

God, please fill my life with people who will show me how to love and serve You. Amen.

The Kuiper (KY-purr) Belt is an icy ring that sits outside of Neptune's orbit and is home to Pluto and lots of other KBOs. (That's scientific talk for Kuiper Belt Objects.) One of them, Eris, is a little smaller than Pluto and has its own moon. Arrokoth is red and shaped like a snowman. And Haumea is shaped like a deflated football and spins end over end every few hours.

WORKING TOGETHER

Be good servants and use your
gifts to serve each other.

1 PETER 4:10 ICB

In Mozambique, Africa, there's a crazy conversation going on—between birds and humans! For the Yao (YOW) people, honey is an important part of their diet. They depend on honeyguide birds to guide them to it. Using a special *brrr-hm* call, the people tell the birds they're ready to go honey hunting. The birds lead the way, chattering at the people to keep up.

Once the beehives are spotted—usually high up in the trees—the Yao climb up, calm the bees with smoke, bust open the hives, and scoop out the honey. Then the birds swoop in to snap up the yummy (to them!) wax and the larvae. Without the birds, the Yao couldn't find the beehives. And without the Yao, the birds couldn't get past the bees to get their treats.

This is called a mutualistic (MYOO-choo-uh-lis-tik) interaction. That means they help each other out. Scientists think the birds are born knowing how to do this. In other words, God created honeyguides and people to work together. Kind of like how He made all of us to work together.

Everyone has something to offer. Think about your friends. Maybe someone knows sports and can explain the rules. Or your math-genius friend can solve the super-tricky problems. Or someone who is extra good at encouraging can lift you up on a tough day. When we use our gifts to work together, we create something better than we could on our own—and that points to the goodness of God!

God, show me how to use the gifts You've given me so I can show Your goodness to the world. Amen.

EXPLORE THE WONDER

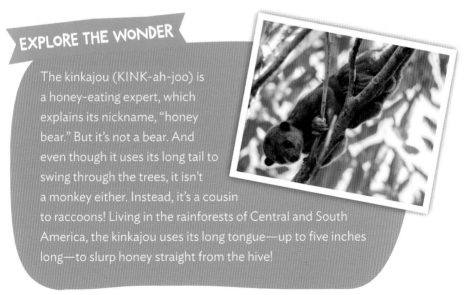

The kinkajou (KINK-ah-joo) is a honey-eating expert, which explains its nickname, "honey bear." But it's not a bear. And even though it uses its long tail to swing through the trees, it isn't a monkey either. Instead, it's a cousin to raccoons! Living in the rainforests of Central and South America, the kinkajou uses its long tongue—up to five inches long—to slurp honey straight from the hive!

COUGH DROP, ANYONE?

"A good person has good things saved
up in his heart. And so he brings
good things out of his heart."

LUKE 6:45 ICB

With its round ears, black button nose, and thick gray and white fur, the koala looks like a teddy bear that's come to life. But even though it's often called a koala *bear*, the koala isn't a bear. It's a marsupial (mar-SOO-pee-uhl), just like the kangaroo.

Koalas only live in one place in the world: Australia. They spend most of their lives—as much as 22 hours a day—sleeping in eucalyptus trees. It's a pretty convenient location because eucalyptus leaves are the *only* thing they eat. No berries, no seeds, no nuts. Just eucalyptus leaves.

The thing is, eucalyptus leaves have a very strong smell. In fact, the oils from these leaves are often used to make cough drops, so you might have smelled their sharp scent before. Because koalas eat so many eucalyptus leaves, they sometimes smell like furry little cough drops!

What goes in *will* come out. It's true for koalas and their cough-drop scent, and it's true for us too. I don't mean you'll smell like that pizza you ate. But if you put things like anger, jealousy, gossip, or hate in your heart, guess what's going to come out in your words and actions? That same nasty stuff. But when you put the love, joy, and kindness of Christ in your heart, then those things will come out—and they "smell" pretty sweet!

God, help me get rid of all the unpleasant things in my heart and mind, and fill me with Your love instead. Amen.

EXPLORE THE WONDER

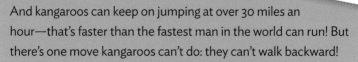

Kangaroos belong to the family *Macropodidae*, which means "big feet." Those big feet help kangaroos jump up to six feet in the air and as far as 25 feet or more in a single bound. And kangaroos can keep on jumping at over 30 miles an hour—that's faster than the fastest man in the world can run! But there's one move kangaroos can't do: they can't walk backward!

GLOWING SEAS?!

The Son reflects the glory of God. He
is an exact copy of God's nature.

HEBREWS 1:3 ICB

For centuries, sailors have talked about mysterious, glowing milky seas. And for centuries, scientists thought these stories were just spooky tall tales—until recently.

In 1995, the SS *Lima* was sailing through the Indian Ocean near Somalia. Suddenly, the sailors found themselves surrounded by glowing waters. In 2005, scientists decided to check out their story using pictures taken by space satellites—and it was true! The glow spread out over almost 6,000 square miles. That's almost 3,000,000 football fields!

What caused that glow? About 40 billion trillion bioluminescent (bahy-oh-loo-muh-NES-uhnt) bacteria called *Vibrio harveyi*, give or take a billion or two. Bioluminescent means these bacteria create their own light. Scientists think they glow in order to attract fish. They actually *want* to be eaten. Because for these bacteria, there's no place they'd rather be than in a fish's gut where they can easily multiply. Home sweet . . . home? *Eww!*

Sailors have been talking about glowing seas since the 1600s, but scientists didn't believe them. At least not until they had photographic proof. They had to see it with their own eyes. Here's the thing: we can't see God with our own eyes right now. But we don't have to see Him to know He's real.

EXPLORE THE WONDER

For centuries, sailors saw what no one else had seen. What things can you discover that no one else has seen? Grab a magnifying glass and head out on an adventure in your own backyard or neighborhood. (Get a parent's permission first!) Look at the big and the small—from birds' feathers to pebbles to towering trees. What in God's wonderful world can you see? Be scientific about it and record your discoveries in a journal.

That's because we can see all the light and love God poured into this world through Jesus—in the way He helped others, the way He welcomed little children, and the way He stills loves even the most unlovable people. When we help, welcome, and love others, we shine some of that same heavenly light and love into this dark world.

God, thank You for Jesus—and for all the ways He helps me see who You really are. Amen.

53

A HEAVENLY GUIDE

"The Helper will teach you everything. He will cause you to remember all the things I told you. This Helper is the Holy Spirit whom the Father will send in my name."

JOHN 14:26 ICB

GPS—it's practically everywhere these days. It's on our smart-phones, in our cars, and even on some watches! It tells us where we are and how to get to where we want to go. But what exactly is GPS?

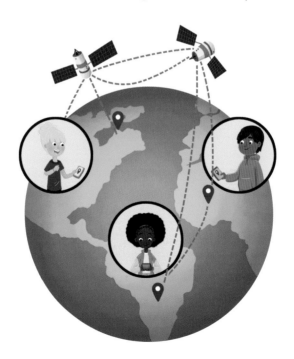

It stands for Global Positioning System. And it's this really cool way to figure out where things are on Earth. Over 95 navigation satellites circle our planet and send out signals. A GPS receiver—like a smartphone—listens for those signals. When it receives, or catches, the signals of at least four different satellites, it can figure out exactly where you are—sometimes within just a few inches! The GPS then uses that information to guide us to where we want to go.

Want to know something even more amazing? When you choose to follow God, He gives you a guide that's better than any GPS. You might say it's God's Positioning System. It—or rather, *He*—is the Holy Spirit. He's God's own Spirit, and He comes to live inside you to help you live the way God wants you to live. The Holy Spirit can tell you exactly where you are in your walk with God and how to get closer to Him. Instead of satellites, He uses God's Word and people to tell you which direction to go. And His directions are perfect every time. Listen to the Holy Spirit, and He'll guide you all the way home to heaven!

God, thank You for sending the Holy Spirit to guide and help me. Teach me to listen to what He tells me about You. Amen.

EXPLORE THE WONDER

Space is huge, but it's getting a little full up there, especially close to Earth. In April 2020, there were 2,666 working satellites in space (and thousands more dead ones). Hundreds more are launching every year for things like communications, the internet, security, and keeping an electronic eye on the environment.

54

DON'T FORGET!

"I will not forget you."

ISAIAH 49:15 ICB

What's the best day you've ever had? Maybe it was a trip to the amusement park, camping with friends, or a day with your grandparents. What do you remember about that day? If you're like me, you remember all the foods you ate, the stuff you saw, and even how the air smelled. It was the best day ever, and you don't want to forget a thing!

How about that big test last week? Do you still remember the fourth US president? Or the answer to 11 x 12? Why are some things easier to remember?

Your brain decides what information to keep and what to toss. It uses short-term memory to remember stuff for a short time. And long-term memory to remember stuff for . . . *wait for it* . . . a long time. The things that interest you are more likely to get put into long-term memory.

That explains why Jesus remembers the people others forget—because He's interested in everyone. Like blind Bartimaeus. When he called out to Jesus for help, everyone around shushed him. *That's just old Bartimaeus*, they thought. They were used to seeing him blind and begging. They forgot he was a real person with hopes and dreams just like them. But Jesus didn't forget Bartimaeus; He healed him (Mark 10:46–52).

Are there people you're forgetting? The homeless person on the corner. That kid who's always picked last for teams. The older person at church who sits alone. Who can you remember and help today?

Lord, thank You for always remembering me. Please show me who I need to remember today. Amen.

Do you remember what you had for breakfast yesterday? Last week? How about three years, two months, and four days ago? Some people do! It's called hyperthymesia (HI-per-thigh-MEE-zee-uh), and it only happens to about 30 or so people in the whole world. These people remember every little thing that's happened to them since they were about 10 years old. Some can even remember things that happened when they were a baby!

IT'S AN INVASION!

Accept God's salvation to be your helmet.

EPHESIANS 6:17 ICB

Pythons are taking over! Florida, that is. The Burmese python usually lives in Southeast Asia, but researchers believe they arrived in Florida in the 1980s. Now tens of thousands—or more—have invaded the Everglades' swamp waters. *Yikes!*

The python's black, tan, and brown skin blends perfectly into the swamps—making them impossible to see. They have no predators, and since one female can lay as many as 50 to 100 eggs every year, you've got a recipe for big trouble.

And I mean *big* trouble! Pythons can grow to 26 feet long and weigh 200 pounds. They'll eat anything they can wrap their massive jaws around. Rabbits and foxes have been wiped out in the Everglades. Raccoons, opossums, and bobcats are dangerously close to disappearing too. These invading snakes are completely changing the environment of the Everglades—for the worse!

But the python isn't the most dangerous invader around. The devil is! He tries to invade your thoughts with lies about who God is, who you are, and how you should live. That's why God gives us the helmet of salvation (Ephesians 6:10–18). Just like a bicycle helmet protects your head, the helmet of salvation uses God's truth to protect your thoughts from the devil's lies. Because the truth is that God loves you so much that He sent Jesus to save you. If you ever feel your thoughts being invaded by the devil's nasty invading lies, pop on the helmet of salvation—and those lies will bounce right off of you!

Lord, when the devil tries to invade my thoughts, remind me to put on the helmet of salvation. Protect me with Your truth. Amen.

EXPLORE THE WONDER

The Burmese python problem started with pets. It's illegal now, but selling pythons for pets was once a huge business in Florida. When pet pythons grew too big, owners released them into the swamps. Then, in August 1992, Hurricane Andrew destroyed a building holding hundreds of pythons and other snakes. They also escaped into the swamps, and that's when the number of snakes really exploded!

WHEN THE EARTH MOVED

Do not forget to do good to others. And
share with them what you have.

HEBREWS 13:16 ICB

Imagine: It's the early 1800s, and you're one of the few settlers in the wilderness of Tennessee. Suddenly the ground begins to shake. Huge slabs of earth rise up and smash down. Trees topple like toothpicks. And the nearby Mississippi River jumps up over 15 feet in the air and falls back again.

That's what happened between December 1811 and March 1812. A series of violent earthquakes ripped open a crater 20 miles long and seven miles wide in the corner of Tennessee. They caused the Mississippi River to flow backward for several hours, filling in the crater and creating Reelfoot Lake.

Today, Reelfoot Lake is one of the most beautiful places on Earth. Bald cypress trees rise up out of the water, while a forest of stumps hides just underneath the surface. The area is rich with all kinds of plants, flowers, waterfowl (birds that live near the water), and majestic American bald eagles.

Reelfoot Lake, Tennessee

So much beauty came out of that terrible disaster.

But the greatest beauty that comes out of any disaster is the way God's people love and help those who are hurting. You might wonder, *What can I do?* But helping even one person makes a huge difference. The next time a disaster strikes, decide to help. Collect coins by doing a coin drive. Help pack up boxes of supplies. Collect food. And most of all, pray. God will hear you, and He'll help you help others—and that's even more beautiful than Reelfoot Lake.

God, when a disaster hits, remind me to first stop and talk to You. Show me how I can help others. Amen.

EXPLORE THE WONDER

Though the Richter (RIHK-ter) scale, which measures earthquakes, wasn't invented until 1935, scientists think the Reelfoot quakes may have measured as high as 8.8. (The most powerful ever recorded was a 9.5 in Chile in 1960.) The quakes were so strong that President James Madison and his wife, Dolly, felt the tremors in the White House, over 850 miles away! Church bells rang in Boston, and shaking was even reported 1,200 miles away in Canada!

IT'S ABOUT TIME

Live wisely. Use every chance
you have for doing good.

EPHESIANS 5:15–16 NCV

What is a day? It's one sunrise and one sunset. Right? Well, sort of. We think of one cycle of daytime and nighttime as a day—24 hours. And it is. That's called a solar day. But a day can also be the amount of time it takes for the Earth to spin completely around on its axis one time. That's called a sidereal (si-DEER-ee-uhl) day. Earth's sidereal day is 23 hours, 56 minutes, and 4.1 seconds long. It's about four minutes shorter than a solar

Earth

Jupiter

Venus

Neptune

day. That means that for the Earth to turn all the way back to facing the Sun again, it would need to spin for four more minutes.

But that's only true here on Earth. If you were to visit Jupiter, you'd have to work really fast to get a day's work done. That's because a day on Jupiter only lasts about 10 hours. A day on Venus is 5,832 hours, or 243 Earth days! And on Neptune, one year is 60,190 days—or over 164 Earth years. Imagine living on Neptune and waiting for your birthday to roll around!

Sometimes it seems like time flies by, and other times it moves *sooo* slowly. But the fact is that every day on Earth is 24 hours long. Give or take four minutes. What are you doing with your 24 hours? Don't waste it. Use it wisely. Challenge yourself to do these things every day: help someone, encourage someone, exercise, rest, play, laugh, and most importantly, spend time with God. Don't miss out on a chance to do good!

God, remind me each morning to spend my 24 hours in ways that will honor You. Amen.

EXPLORE THE WONDER

Ticktock, ticktock. Older clocks tell time by counting the number of times a pendulum moves back and forth. Newer clocks and wristwatches track how often quartz crystals vibrate to determine the time. But atomic clocks—the most accurate clocks invented—use atomic time. That means they count how many times a cesium (SEE-zee-uhm) atom vibrates. And it vibrates 9,192,631,770 times per second!

58

DON'T DO IT!

"If people love me, they will obey my teaching."

JOHN 14:23 NCV

D on't turn the page! Seriously—don't do it! You *don't* want to see the picture on the next page.

Okay, how many of you turned the page? Yeah, I took a quick peek too. And I already knew what's there! Why do we sometimes do the very thing we're told not to do? It's called *rebellion*. It means to disobey. It first showed up when God told Adam and Eve, "Don't eat that fruit." What did they do? They ate it. Sure, the devil tempted them. But he didn't stuff it in their mouths. They *chose* to rebel.

When we get upset, angry, or annoyed because rules keep us from doing what we want to do, that's called psychological reactance (sie-kuh-LOJ-i-kuhl ree-AK-tuhns). It can make us want to rebel and break the rules, just because we don't want someone else telling us what to do. It's kind of like when the teacher says don't get out of your seat, and then all you can think about is why you need to get out of your seat.

Here's the thing about rules, though, especially God's rules. They're there to protect us and help us live the best possible lives. Like when God told Adam and Eve not to eat that fruit. He knew it would bring sin and death and all kinds of trouble into the world. God's rules are always good because He is always good. So when He says to do something—like don't lie, don't cheat or steal, and love your neighbor—don't rebel. Trust that God only wants what's best for you.

Lord, I want to love and obey You always. Help me to know and follow Your rules and trust that they are for my good. Amen.

EXPLORE THE WONDER

Is there a rule you don't like to obey? Maybe it's at school, at home, or out in the world. Let's do some thinking about that rule. Who made it? Does it help or protect someone (even if it's not you)? Does it line up with God's rules? Before you decide to rebel, do some thinking—and praying—first.

59

WHISPERS AND WHISKERS

*After the earthquake there was a fire, but the L*ORD *was not in the fire. And after the fire there was the sound of a gentle whisper.*

1 KINGS 19:12 NLT

Cats have them. Dogs have them. And rats definitely have them. So do squirrels, deer, sea lions, walruses, and even manatees. What are they? Whiskers! Almost every mammal has whiskers, except just a very few—like the platypus, spiny anteater, and us!

The scientific term for whiskers is *vibrissae* (vi-BRIS-ee), and each one is full of nerves. A single cat's whisker has up to 200 nerve cells, but one seal's whisker has over 1,500! When whiskers brush against something or when air or water moves over them, those nerves pick up all kinds of information about the size, shape, location, and movement of whatever they're touching. That's especially important in places where it's dark and hard for the animals to see.

Whiskers softly and quietly help animals find their way. God does the same for us. He guides us—not with whiskers but with whispers. Like He did for Elijah the prophet. Elijah was exhausted and scared because he was running away from Queen Jezebel, who wanted him dead (1 Kings 18–19). So God sent Elijah up on a mountain. First, a massive wind blew through. Then came an earthquake and a fire. Last came a soft, gentle whisper, and that's when God told Elijah which way to go.

Sometimes God does speak loudly. But usually He whispers—through His Word, His people, and the Holy Spirit—to help us find our way.

God, help me take time today to be still and quiet so I can hear Your whispers and not miss a thing. Show me what You have next for me. Amen.

EXPLORE THE WONDER

If you want to know how a cat is feeling, check out her whiskers. When she's happy, her whiskers will stick out sideways and droop down just a bit. If she's curious or excited, they'll be fanned out in front of her. But if her whiskers are folded back flat against her face, watch out! She's either mad or scared, and she's ready to attack!

60

DON'T SLIP DOWN THAT SLOPE!

He lifted me out of the pit of
destruction, out of the sticky mud.

PSALM 40:2 ICB

Carnivores (KAHR-nuh-vohrs) are animals like lions, wolves, and sharks that eat meat. But what about plants? Yep! Plants can be carnivores too. Travel to Australia, Madagascar, or Southeast Asia, and you'll find meat-eating tropical pitcher plants!

Some of this plant's leaves look pretty ordinary, but others grow into vase-shaped pitchers. That entire pitcher is a trap! The lid lures insects in with yummy-smelling nectar. The cup is often the color of the rotten meat insects

love to eat. The rim (or top edge) of the cup is waxy and super-slippery. So when bugs creep or fly in looking for a treat, they slide down the pitcher's waxy throat into a pool of sticky liquid. Then it's lunchtime for the plant!

The pitcher plant's trap is a lot like the one the devil uses. I mean, he doesn't say, "Hey, look at this big, terrible, stinky sin. Want some?" No, the devil lures you in with something small that doesn't seem like a big deal and looks good. Maybe it's a "little" fib to get you out of trouble. Or a "little" cheating to get a good grade. Or a "little" talking back to your parents because the kids on TV do. But that little sin is a slippery slope. Soon you're sliding down into bigger and bigger sins until you're stuck in a sticky pool of sin.

Here's the good news, though: God will rescue you. Tell Him you're sorry and ask Him to help—He always will. But trust me, life is so much better and easier if you just don't slide down that slope.

God, when sin starts to look sweet, please give me the wisdom to see the truth and the strength to say no to sin. Amen.

EXPLORE THE WONDER

Some insects and other animals actually live *inside* pitcher plants. Spiders can hide under the lid to catch unsuspecting insects. Frogs will creep down inside the cup to snap up flies that come buzzing down inside. And some species of pitcher plants even attract tree shrews and bats—not to eat them but to collect their nutrient-rich poo! *Eww!*

61

STORMS ON THE SUN

When you are angry, do not sin. And
do not go on being angry all day.

EPHESIANS 4:26 ICB

I f the Sun is shining, the weather isn't stormy, right? Well, that's true on Earth. But on the Sun? That's a different story.

From down here on Earth, the Sun looks pretty calm. But as it turns out, the Sun is a stormy place filled with solar storms, which begin with huge explosions called solar flares. These flares are more powerful than a million nuclear bombs exploding at the same time! Solar flares are often followed by CMEs, or coronal (KOR-uh-null) mass ejections. CMEs shoot out streams of electrical charges that zoom toward Earth at over three million miles per hour!

Solar storms happen a lot more often than we realize. There are times when several storms happen in a single day and other times when CMEs don't occur for days. Most solar storms are harmless, but the most powerful ones can knock out radio signals and communications, like cell phones.

The Sun can blast out solar storms and get away with it. But if *we* allow our anger to explode out, we're headed for trouble. Sure, things go wrong and people do wrong, and there are times to be angry. But be extra careful about what you do and say when you're angry. "Blasting" someone can interrupt your communication. In other words, it can hurt your relationships with the people you care about. So take a deep breath. Walk away for a minute. Think—and pray—before you speak. And leave the storms to the Sun.

Lord, when I am angry, please bless me with Your wisdom so I can see clearly what I need to do. Amen.

In 1859, an amateur astronomer named Richard Carrington became the first person to witness and record a solar flare. Carrington was looking through his telescope and saw bright white light erupt from dark spots on the Sun. Just a few hours later, the solar storm hit Earth, knocking out telegraph communications and lighting up the night skies. It became known as the Carrington Event—the largest solar storm ever recorded.

SPEAK UP!

Speak up for those who cannot
speak for themselves.

PROVERBS 31:8 ICB

Say something out loud. Anything. Like, "I am fearfully and wonder-fully made!" As you speak, put your hand on your throat. Feel that vibration? That vibration creates the sounds we use to talk.

It all starts in your larynx (LAR-ingks)—or voice box. This small hollow tube is made out of cartilage (KAHR-tl-ij), just like your ears and the end of

vocal folds

your nose. It sits on top of the windpipe in your throat. The larynx has folds of membranes (like thin bands of tissue) attached to it. They're called vocal folds, or vocal cords. When the air from your lungs pushes past those vocal folds, they vibrate and make the sounds we use for talking. They vibrate when you talk, sing, or even yell, but not when you whisper. Try it out. Hold your hand over your throat while you whisper. There's no vibration, right?

If you want to make a difference in this world—if you want the world to "vibrate" because of what you say and do—you need to speak up. Just whispering won't do it. Use your voice to make things better. The Bible tells us to speak up for those who can't speak for themselves, like speaking up for that younger kid who's being picked on. Or it could mean speaking up for animals that can't defend themselves against poachers, or speaking up to protect the Earth from pollution. So speak up! Then put your words into actions and make a difference in this world.

Dear God, please give me the courage to speak up, knowing my words make a difference, and give me the wisdom to know what to say. Amen.

EXPLORE THE WONDER

A talking elephant? Yep! Koshik, an Asian elephant, "speaks" by using his trunk to change the shape of his mouth. As a young elephant at the Everland Zoo in South Korea, Koshik began imitating the words of his keepers. Koshik can say *hello*, *sit down*, *no*, *lie down*, and *good*. But scientists don't believe he knows what he's saying. I wonder what Koshik would say about that.

AN OCTOPUS GARDEN

"If two or three people come together
in my name, I am there with them."

MATTHEW 18:20 ICB

Gardens are for growing corn, flowers, and octopuses. *Octopuses?!* Well, sort of. Off the coast of California, scientists discovered a garden of octopuses—or octopi, if you want to be fancy about it.

In 2018, scientists were exploring the Monterey Bay National Marine Sanctuary, using special underwater robots. That's when they discovered an octopus garden, or nursery—the largest ever found! Over 1,000 female octopuses were brooding. (*Brooding* means taking care of their eggs.) Scientists wondered why they choose that spot. After all, it was over two miles deep where it's usually freezing cold. That's when scientists saw the shimmer.

You've probably seen the shimmer too. Maybe on a road on a hot summer's day. It happens when the Sun heats the pavement, and the pavement heats the air around it. The warm air isn't as dense as the other air. So when light passes through it, it bounces around, causing the shimmer. When scientists saw that shimmer in the water, they knew it was warmer there—probably because of an underground volcano. Instead of a frigid 35 degrees Fahrenheit, it was a warm 50 degrees, perfect for an octopus garden.

We may not be two miles under the ocean, but when we gather with those who love Jesus, we have our own shimmer of warmth—the love and presence of Jesus. That's because Jesus promises that whenever two or more gather together to pray and praise Him, He is right there with us. So grab a friend or two, and enjoy the shimmer of being with Jesus!

Jesus, thank You for coming to be with Your people. Help me soak up the warmth of Your love and share it with the world around me. Amen.

EXPLORE THE WONDER

Monterey Bay National Marine Sanctuary is also home to an amazing variety of sponges—not the scrubbing kind! These sponges are very simple underwater animals. They can't move, so they trap their food from the water that moves through them. Sponges come in so many shapes, colors, and sizes, including some that look like fans, twigs, and even fancy goblets!

64

IS THERE LiFE OuT THERE?

We know that in everything God works
for the good of those who love him.

ROMANS 8:28 ICB

On July 30, 2020, NASA launched a robotic science rover, Perseverance, into space on a mission to Mars. Sounds like something out of a movie, right? It's not! Over six months after it left Earth, Perseverance landed on February 18, 2021.

Perseverance is about the size of a car, and it's searching for signs of life on Mars. No, not little green aliens. Perseverance is studying the rocks and dirt in a spot called the Jezero (YEH-zuh-doh) Crater. Scientists believe the crater was once filled with water—and maybe even microscopic life. Perseverance is using two special tools called SHERLOC and WATSON (Don't recognize those names? Ask a grown-up!) to take samples and pictures of the rocks.

When you think about life on Mars, microscopic clues in rocks probably aren't what you imagine. And just like on Mars, life on Earth can look *very* different from what we imagine. I don't mean we suddenly turn green or grow weird tentacles. It's just that life doesn't always go the way we plan. Sometimes we get surprised, and not in a good way. Here's the thing, though: God is *never* surprised. He already knows everything that will happen—the good, bad, and completely crazy. God gave us the Bible to show us how He works in people's lives and how He can bring something good out of everything that happens when we trust Him. With God, there's always a beautiful life out there.

God, You are never surprised. Please guide each step of my life and use everything to bring about something good. Amen.

EXPLORE THE WONDER

NASA's Perseverance rover landed on Mars with a helicopter nicknamed Ingenuity (in-juh-NOO-i-tee) strapped to its belly. Scientists wanted to know if it could fly in Mars's thin atmosphere. Ingenuity was designed to fly for 90 seconds, going as high as 15 feet and traveling about 980 feet total. During Ingenuity's fifth flight, it flew 423 feet at an altitude of 16 feet. The trip lasted 108 seconds, but before it landed, it rose to 33 feet and took photos of its surroundings!

65

PERFECTLY IMPERFECT

*The Lord's love never ends. His mercies
never stop. They are new every morning.*

LAMENTATIONS 3:22-23 ICB

Many years ago, people believed the Earth was flat. But thanks to the ancient Greeks, we've long known that the Earth is round. Aristotle figured it out by watching the stars. And Eratosthenes—let's just call him Mr. E—measured the angle of the Sun in two different cities, did some extra-fancy math, and declared the Earth was definitely round. And that was over 2,000 years ago! But is the Earth *really* round?

Not exactly. It's round-*ish*. It's a sphere, like a ball, but it's not a perfect sphere. As the Earth rotates (or spins) in space, it puts pressure on the north and south poles. That pressures flattens them just a bit. It also makes the equator bulge slightly. But even though the Earth isn't perfectly round, it's a perfectly wonderful place for us to live.

That's kind of like us. I mean, none of us is perfect. We lose our temper and yell at a sibling, roll our eyes at our parents, or make a promise and don't keep it. The good news is that God doesn't expect us to be perfect. And He gives us a way to bounce back from all those "imperfect things" we do. It's called mercy, and basically, it means we get a second chance—to apologize to the person we wronged and to God. As soon as you realize you've messed up, ask God to forgive you. Because His mercy is new every morning—and every time you say you're sorry.

God, help me to see my sins and mistakes. Please forgive me, and then give me the strength to make them right. Amen.

EXPLORE THE WONDER

Long ago scientists and explorers used shadows, stars, and even lunar eclipses to figure out that the Earth was round. Today's scientists use geodesy (jee-AH-dus-see). It's a branch of science that uses GPS and information from satellites to measure things like the Earth's shape, gravity, and how fast it spins in space. And all that science says the Earth is round. Well, round-ish.

66

FEEL THAT SMELL?

We are the sweet smell of Christ
among those who are being saved and
among those who are being lost.

2 CORINTHIANS 2:15 ICB

When you catch a whiff of freshly baked cookies, what's the first thing you remember? What's the first thing you feel? How about when you smell Play-Doh? Or that slightly weird "old sneakers and mystery meat" smell on the first day of school? Certain smells can make us remember and feel so much.

It starts with our noses, of course. The things we smell, or scents, are actually made up of tiny little particles. We breathe them in through the nose. And that's when it gets interesting. You see, whenever we taste, touch, see, or

Thalamus

Hippocampus

Amygdala

hear something, that information goes to a part of the brain called the thalamus (THAL-uh-muhs). From there, the brain decides what to do with that information. But smells skip all that and go straight to the brain's amygdala (uh-MIG-duh-luh) where emotions are sorted out. Then it zips over to the hippocampus (hip-uh-KAM-puhs)—which oddly enough has nothing to do with hippos and everything to do with remembering. That's why smells are so connected to our feelings and memories.

When you love Jesus and try to love others the way He did, your life "smells" sweet to those around you. Just like a scent that stirs up good feelings and memories, how you live your life helps people feel loved. It helps them remember God and His promises. And it helps them follow Him. So what can you do to smell sweet today?

Lord, help me live well so my life "smells" sweet to You and everyone around me. Amen.

EXPLORE THE WONDER

Babies can smell even before they're born. The baby's nose begins forming at around six or seven weeks with its first olfactory neurons, which help with identifying odors. At about 10 weeks, his or her nose can feel touches. By the eighth month—or perhaps even as early as the sixth—babies can smell inside the womb. What do they smell? Whatever mom eats, especially vanilla and strong-smelling foods like garlic.

67

IT'S POSSIBLE

Nothing will be impossible with God.

LUKE 1:37 ESV

What do you get if you combine a duck, an otter, and a beaver? No, it's not the next mutant superhero. It's a platypus! This creature is so bizarre that when scientists saw the body of one for the first time, they thought it wasn't a real animal!

With the bill and webbed feet of a duck, the body and fur of an otter, and the tail of a beaver, the platypus is one strange-looking animal. This Australian mammal is graceful in the water, but it waddles a bit on land. For food, it dives underwater and uses its bill to scoop up insects, worms, larvae, and shellfish, along with some mud and gravel. (Because the platypus doesn't have teeth, it uses the mud and gravel to grind up its food.) Unlike most mammals, the platypus lays eggs. And if this animal wasn't weird enough already, its back feet point backward!

Scientists first thought an animal with a duck's bill and a beaver's tail couldn't possibly be real. But just because something *seems* impossible doesn't mean it is. Especially when it comes to God. He does lots of things that can be hard to believe. Like talking through a burning bush to Moses (Exodus 3:2), shutting those lions' mouths to keep Daniel safe (Daniel 6:22), or walking on the stormy water like it was a sidewalk (Matthew 14:25). All of those things are 100 percent true! God makes the impossible possible (Mark 10:27). The next time you think something about God can't possibly be true, remember the platypus and know there's nothing God can't do!

God, You've made so many amazing things. But nothing is as amazing as You, the One who created it all! There's nothing You can't do. Amen.

EXPLORE THE WONDER

The okapi looks like a zebra, donkey, deer, and antelope all squashed together into one animal! Nicknamed the African unicorn, the rare okapi is a relative of the giraffe and lives in the Ituri Forest, a rainforest in Africa. Its tongue is so long— up to 18 inches—that it can lick its own ears and eyelids!

68

HUNGRY, HUNGRY HiPPO

A person does not live on bread alone,
but by everything the LORD says.

DEUTERONOMY 8:3 NCV

Did you ever play that game called Hungry Hungry Hippos? Well, as it turns out, hippos do get really hungry! And since they're roughly the weight of three small cars, it takes a lot to fill them up. They eat

about 80 pounds of food a night. (That's like eating over 320 burgers a day!) They spend about four to six hours a night chowing down.

I say "night" because hippos do their munching at night. Because they live in the heat of Africa, they spend their days mostly in the water. They slip out at night, when it's cooler, to graze for food. In the dark, a hippo's super-sensitive ears can hear fruit falling to the ground, and their noses help them sniff it out. Hippos prefer to eat near the water, but they will sometimes travel miles to find enough to eat.

When hippos get hungry, they go where they need to go and take the time they need to eat. We do the same thing when our tummies get rumbly. But our stomachs aren't the only part of us that needs "food." Our hearts, minds, and souls get hungry too—hungry for God's truth. His Word is called the Bread of Life, and it keeps us strong so we can stand up for what's right. It also fills us up with His goodness so we're not tempted to get full on things that are bad for us. So be sure to grab a "slice" of God's Word every day. A verse or chapter a day will keep the hunger away!

Hippos spend almost all their daytime hours in the water. They even sleep underwater, just bobbing to the top every few minutes to take a breath, then sinking back down again, without ever waking up! So hippos are probably amazing swimmers, right? No! Hippos can't swim. They can't even float. Instead, they sort of tiptoe across the river bottom—like humongous underwater ballerinas.

Dear God, please make me hungry for Your Word and teach me to fill myself up with Your truth every day. Amen.

69

EARTH'S TRAVEL BUDDY

Seek [God's] will in all you do, and he
will show you which path to take.

PROVERBS 3:6 NLT

Did you know Earth has a travel buddy as it makes its trip around the Sun? And I don't mean the Moon. This travel buddy is named Cruithne (*KROO-ee-nyuh*). It was discovered in the 1980s, and for a while, people thought it might be Earth's second moon. But moons—like our Moon—orbit around their planet, and Cruithne orbits around the Sun instead. Cruithne is actually an asteroid about three miles wide.

Why did people think it might be a second moon? Because its path around the Sun is a lot like Earth's. But while Earth's orbit is round, Cruithne's is kind of bean-shaped. So sometimes it's closer to Earth and sometimes it's farther away. Think of it as two cars traveling side by side—except sometimes Cruithne turns onto a different road and then later joins back up beside Earth again. That's called a co-orbital configuration, or as I like to say, traveling with a buddy.

Do you have a travel buddy? Someone who helps you figure out which way to go in life? Parents and family make great travel buddies, but they can't go on every trip with you. Friends sometimes take a different road. Want to know the perfect travel buddy? God! You can ask Him for directions, tell Him all your stories, sing songs, and just enjoy having Someone to share the trip with. And with God as your travel buddy, you know you'll always be headed the right way.

God, I'm so glad I get to travel through life with You. Thank You for always being my travel buddy! Amen.

EXPLORE THE WONDER

Earth has at least one other travel buddy. It goes by the fancy name of Asteroid 2002 AA29. This roughly 200-foot-wide chunk of space rock follows a racetrack-shaped orbit around the Sun, similar to that of the Earth. But don't expect to see it up in the sky anytime soon. Asteroid 2002 AA29 gets close to Earth every 95 years, so it won't be back until 2098!

FILL UP WITH THE GOOD STUFF

"A person does not live only by eating bread.
But a person lives by everything the Lord says."

MATTHEW 4:4 ICB

From oysters to squirrels to lions, all of God's creatures have to eat—including us! And while oysters might enjoy chowing down on just plankton and algae, we need to eat a variety of foods to get all the

nutrients (NOO-tree-ents) our bodies need. Nutrients are the good stuff we get from the food we eat, like vitamins, minerals, and proteins.

Not all foods have the good stuff, though. Junk foods, like chips and sweets, have hardly any nutrients. To get everything your body needs, eat foods from each of the five food groups every day: grains (like bread and rice), dairy (like milk and cheese), fruits (like apples, kiwis, and bananas), vegetables (like carrots and broccoli), and protein (like meats and eggs). Eating these good foods not only keeps our bodies strong, but it also helps us have more energy, be happier, sleep better, and even remember better.

EXPLORE THE WONDER

Food just tastes better when you help cook it. So plan your own meal! Choose foods from each of the five food groups. Feed your soul, too, by picking a Bible verse to go with your meal. With a grown-up's help, fix and serve that meal to your family. If you can, make extra to share with a friend or neighbor.

Our souls need good food too. And just like we need nutrients from a variety of food groups, our souls need a variety of spiritual "foods." We get hungry for God's Word, which keeps our faith strong and growing. We also need plenty of prayer to get us through the day and help us sleep at night. Praising God chases sadness away. Singing fills us up with comfort and joy. And fellowship—being with God's people—gives us the strength, energy, and encouragement to keep loving and following Him. So go ahead—fill up with the good stuff! You wouldn't forget to feed your body every day, so don't forget to feed your soul too!

Lord, thank You for all the good things You give us to eat. Thank You most of all for Your Word that feeds my soul. Amen.

BIG LITTLE THINGS

"If you are faithful in little things, you
will be faithful in large ones."

LUKE 16:10 NLT

Toes! They wiggle, and they get tickled. And if you forget to scrub between them, they can get a little smelly. But what are these guys for anyway? Toes keep us on our toes, er, feet. They help us stay balanced. That's because they're the part of our body that touches the ground the most. Want to see how important toes are? Try this: Stand on one foot. Pretty easy, right? Now, lift your toes off the floor. That's much harder!

Toes also help us run faster. When you're running and you put your foot down, your toes help "catch" you and keep you from face-planting. As you pick your feet up, they push off to help you move forward. Just try running with your toes raised up and see how fast you can move!

Toes might be little, but they're big-time important. In fact, little things are often more important than we think. Like all the "little" good things you can do. It's easy to see the big ways others serve God, help others, or take care of our planet and then think only big things matter. But little things add up. Try to help one person every day. Pray for your mom and dad, help a friend who's spilled everything from their bookbag, or pick up the litter that blew into your neighbor's yard. Maybe those things don't seem big to you, but they're big to the one you helped—and they're big to God too. And just think: if you help one different person every day for a year, that's 365 people—and that's pretty big!

God, I know that little things matter to You. Please show me all the big "little" things I can do. Amen.

EXPLORE THE WONDER

Are your toes ticklish? Test it out and see. Tickle your own toes. What? It's not working? As it turns out, we can't tickle ourselves. That's because a big part of being ticklish is being surprised. But there's a part of our brain called the cerebellum (ser-uh-BEL-uhm) that keeps track of all our movements. And it won't let us sneak up on ourselves!

WHAT WOUNDS CAN DO

He heals the brokenhearted and
binds up their wounds.

PSALM 147:3 NIV

If you've ever watched an old western movie, you've probably seen the big, tall cactus with the really long arms. It's called a saguaro (suh-GWAR-oh), and it only grows in the Sonoran Desert in the southwest United Sates.

The saguaro and the Gila (HEE-luh) woodpecker have a special relationship. This zebra-striped little bird pecks out a nest-sized hole in the cactus. Because it's wet and soft inside the cactus, it's not a good nest—yet! So the woodpecker waits about a year. In that time, the cactus's "wound" scabs over and dries out—much like when you skin your knee. This scab is permanent, though, and it creates a safe, cool nest for the woodpecker. Older saguaros might have 20 or more nests! The "wound" that seems painful to the saguaro at first becomes a place of comfort for the woodpecker.

Your wounds can do the same thing. Okay, not *exactly* the same thing. No woodpecker is going to live inside your arm. But when you've been wounded by a lie, gossip, a sickness, or a loss, you understand how it feels to be hurt. As God comforts you, you learn what you need to feel better. Then, when someone else is wounded in the same way, you know how to comfort them. It might be listening to their troubles, inviting them to sit with you on the bus, or writing a note about how much they matter to you. The point is, whenever you're wounded, God can use you to comfort someone else.

God, thank You for Your comfort when I'm hurt. Teach me to use my own hurts to comfort those who are hurting too. Amen.

Elf owl next to a saguaro cactus

Gila woodpeckers only use those saguaro nests for one year. When they move out, other birds move in, like elf owls and purple martins. Even after the saguaro dies, the nests are still useful. The scabbed-over nests become waterproof vessels called "boots." Native Americans once used them to hold drinking water before canteens and water bottles were invented.

ARE YOU BLUE?

Why am I so sad? Why am I so upset? I should
put my hope in God. I should keep praising him.

PSALM 42:5-6 ICB

If you happened to be on the island of Java at night, you might see what looks like eerie blue lava trickling down the side of the Kawah Ijen Volcano. But it's not the lava that's blue. Sulfur gases boil up out of the volcano along with the lava. When those gases hit the air, they burst into blue flames. The flames follow the flow of the lava, making the lava look blue.

The lava is actually a bright golden yellow. That's because the rocks melted by a volcano are rocks of bright yellow sulfur. Miners brave the poisonous gases to harvest it. Once the lava cools into solid sulfur, they break off chunks and carry it back down the mountain to sell. The smell is terrible, and it gets stuck on your clothes, your hair, everything!

When you're feeling down, the "smell" of sadness can get into everything and make your whole world look blue. And let me say that it's okay to be sad when sad things happen. But you don't want to stay that way.

The best way to feel better is to be grateful. Scientific studies have shown that being grateful helps you feel better, sleep better, and be a better friend to the people around you. So the next time you're blue, take a minute to stop and notice all the things God has given you. Things you can see, like family and friends. And things you can't see, like love. Then praise Him for all of them. Because gratitude plus praise chases the blues away.

Lord, when I'm feeling sad and blue, remind me of all the ways I am loved by You. Amen.

EXPLORE THE WONDER

The bright turquoise waters of Lake Kawah Ijen might look like the perfect place to dive in, but don't! Those waters are blue for a reason: metal-dissolving acid. At half a mile across, Kawah Ijen is the world's largest acidic lake. It's also located inside the crater of a volcano. So, yeah, definitely no swimming there!

Sunrise at Lake Kawah Ijen in Indonesia

WHO OWNS THE MOON?

What [God] says he will do, he does.
What he promises, he keeps.

NUMBERS 23:19 ICB

Who owns the Moon? That might seem like a crazy question, but ever since we started looking for a way to get to the Moon, lots of people have been asking it. So back in 1967, some of the world's countries came together to make a treaty, or an agreement. It was called the Treaty on Principles Governing the Activities of States in the Exploration and Use of Outer Space, including the Moon and Other Celestial Bodies. *Whew!*

Thankfully, most people just call it the Outer Space Treaty. It says that space belongs to everybody. So far, 110 nations have signed it, and others are still considering it. (Yes, over 50 years later!)

Sounds like a great treaty, right? There's only one problem. It's weak. A country can just send a letter and get out of it. In other words, these countries made a promise, but they can break it if they want to.

Did you know that God makes a kind of treaty with us? It's called a covenant (KUH-vuh-nuhnt). In this covenant, or promise, God promises that if we believe Jesus is the Son of God, who died for our sins and rose to life—and if we follow Him—our sins will be forgiven. He will send His Holy Spirit to live inside us and guide us. And one day, we will live in heaven with Him forever.

That's God's promise. And the best thing about it is that He will never, ever break it.

Lord, thank You for keeping Your promises, especially the promise that we will one day live with You. How wonderful that will be! Amen.

Planting every nation's flag on the moon—or on other planets—could get cluttered, but there might be a simple solution: an Earth flag! Designed by a Swedish university student, the Earth flag has seven rings to represent each continent. The rings form a shape of a flower, which is a symbol of life, and the blue background represents the color of Earth as seen from space. As we explore the galaxy, we may need to plant only one flag—after all, we're all citizens of Earth!

75

SAY "CHEESE"!

Continue praying and keep alert. And
when you pray, always thank God.

COLOSSIANS 4:2 ICB

Choppers, ivories, fangs. What am I talking about? Teeth! Not all teeth are the same, though. Those incisors (in-SI-zurz) up front are for biting. Canines (KAY-nahynz) are for tearing. And those molars (MOH-lerz) in the back are for grinding. All your teeth are covered with pearly white enamel (ih-NAM-uhl). It's the hardest thing in your body—even stronger than bones. Enamel protects your teeth, but it's still important to take care of them.

premolar

molar

incisor

canine

Here's why: If you break a bone, it'll heal itself. If you skin your knee, your body can take care of that too. But if you chip a tooth or get a cavity, your tooth can't fix itself. You'll need a dentist for that.

Take care of your teeth by brushing for at least two minutes twice each day. And don't forget to floss! Brushing and flossing get rid of the plaque (plak) that "eats away" enamel.

Just as you take care of your teeth every day, you need to take care of your faith too. It's easy to think, *I know Jesus is God's Son, and I know I love Him. So my faith is good.* But no matter how strong your faith is, you need to help it grow stronger every day. That means reading the Bible, talking to God, and finding ways to praise Him. If you're new to spending time with God like that, start with two minutes a day and build up from there. Because even though your teeth are pretty important, your faith matters even more!

God, forgive me for the times I forget to take care of my faith. I want to love You and praise You each and every day. Amen.

EXPLORE THE WONDER

Spit is pretty important stuff. It keeps your mouth moist and comfortable. It's the first step in digesting your food. It even helps heal wounds, stops bad breath, and attacks plaque. Since spit can do all those great things, your body makes a lot of it—about a half-gallon of it every single day!

76

UNICORNS OF THE SEA?

Lord God, you are God, and
your words are true.

2 SAMUEL 7:28 ICB

U nicorns are just fairy tales, right? Maybe not! Take a look at the narwhal (NAR-wall). This massive mammal lives in the Arctic waters around Canada, Greenland, Russia, and Norway. It grows up to 17 feet long, which is like you and three friends all standing on each other's heads. And it weighs up to 4,200 pounds, which is a *lot* more than you and all your friends put together!

The narwhal has a sword-like tusk growing straight out of its head that can grow to 10 feet long! That tusk earned the narwhal its nickname: unicorn of the sea. While there aren't any spiral-horned horses trotting around, maybe the unicorn (which means "one horn" in Latin) isn't a *complete* fairy tale after all.

Some people say the people and places of the Bible are just fairy tales. But biblical archaeologists (ar-key-AH-luh-jists) are digging up things from the past to prove just how real they were. They've found the walls of Jericho that Joshua marched around—or what's left of them (Joshua 6)! They've uncovered the Pool of Siloam where the blind man washed mud from his eyes (John 9). And now they think they've found Peter's house (Luke 4)! The more we explore, the more we find God.

We don't need these discoveries to know God is real. Just one look at the stars tells us only He could make something magnificent like that (Psalm 19:1). But seeing the places where the stories happened helps us know the Bible is so much more than fairy tales.

That long, spiraling tusk sticking out of the narwhal's head is actually a tooth! Usually only male narwhals have a tusk, though about two out of every 100 females has a tusk too. The tusk has up to 10 million nerve endings in it. Scientists aren't sure, but they think the narwhal uses it to find food. Either way, it looks really cool!

God, I know You are real, and I praise You for the real ways You work in this universe and in my life. Amen.

BLOW, DERECHO
WINDS, BLOW

He calmed the storm to a whisper.

PSALM 107:29 NLT

Wind can roar off the ocean in a hurricane or twist itself into a tornado. *Or* it can blow across the land as a derecho (deh-REY-choh) wind. What? You've never heard of derechos? Don't worry—they're pretty rare, so you're not alone.

Unlike tornado winds that continually rotate, derecho winds blow in a straight line. (*Derecho* means "straight ahead" in Spanish.) They form when the wet air of a thunderstorm meets the dry air around it. The water in the air evaporates and cools the air. The cool air is heavier, and it sinks—fast! That creates a powerful wind called a downburst. The downburst sucks in more air and creates even more downbursts.

To be a derecho, a storm must move at least 58 miles per hour, be roughly 50 miles wide or more, and leave behind a path of destruction at least 240 miles long! They don't twist like a tornado, but they can still knock down power lines, topple trees, flip over cars, and level buildings.

When you hear the word *storm*, you probably think of thunderstorms or tornados—not derechos. And when you think about the storms of life, you probably think about really big problems or really bad news. But storms can be all kinds of things. Storms of busyness, of trying to please everyone, of disappointment, or of simply having a rough day. No matter what your storm looks like, God is bigger and stronger. Trust Him to still your storm!

Lord, when storms hit—even storms of good things—please give me the wisdom to know what to do and what not to do. Amen.

EXPLORE THE WONDER

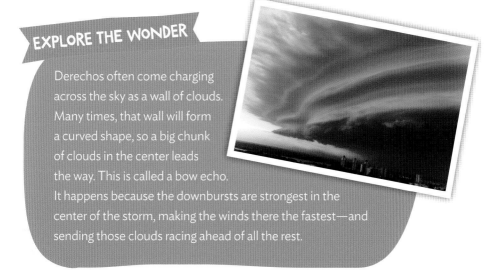

Derechos often come charging across the sky as a wall of clouds. Many times, that wall will form a curved shape, so a big chunk of clouds in the center leads the way. This is called a bow echo. It happens because the downbursts are strongest in the center of the storm, making the winds there the fastest—and sending those clouds racing ahead of all the rest.

 78

ON GUARD!

Carefully guard your thoughts because
they are the source of true life.

PROVERBS 4:23 CEV

Just how smart are smartphones? Well, as it turns out, they're *really* smart. They're even smarter than the computer that first put men on the Moon!

Back in 1969, the *Apollo 11* spacecraft delivered Neil Armstrong and Buzz Aldrin to the Moon. The computer on their spacecraft was the most powerful computer of that time. It was called the Apollo Guidance Computer. And it could hold a whopping 2,048 words in its memory. (That means it could hold less than seven pages of this book in its memory—and that doesn't include the pictures!)

Even today's "dumbest" smartphones have over a million times more memory than the Apollo Guidance Computer. And speed? Today's phones are about 100,000 times faster! How fast is that? Let's just say that even an "old" iPhone 6 could handle about 120 million Moon missions all at the same time—and they're getting smarter and faster every year!

Smartphones *are* really smart. And they can be used for so many good things. Like talking to family and friends, getting directions, looking up Bible verses, and listening to music. But phones can also be dangerous. Songs we shouldn't listen to, games we shouldn't play, and pictures we shouldn't see—they're all just an internet search and a tap or two away. Once you see and hear those things, you can't *unsee* or *unhear* them. Ask your parents to help you set up a filter or an app so you don't accidentally click on the wrong thing. And ask God to keep your thoughts focused on Him, the true source of life. Be on guard—only let the good things get inside your brain.

The first mobile phones were invented back in the 1940s, but they were more like two-way radios or walkie-talkies. Then, in 1973, the first truly mobile phone was made. It was shaped like a brick, weighed almost 2½ pounds, and the battery lasted only about 30 minutes. It could only call—no texting, no music, no pictures!

God, be a fortress around me. Protect my thoughts and my heart from the evil stuff of this world. Amen.

161

DO YOU FEEL IT?

Jesus . . . put his hands on
them and blessed them.

MARK 10:16 ICB

Hard, soft, hot, cold, smooth, or scratchy—how do we know what we're feeling? It all starts with the somatosensory (suh-mat-uh-SEN-suh-ree) system. This system controls your sense of touch. It uses a network of nerve endings and touch receptors in your skin.

Here's how it works: Let's say you reach out and your skin touches something, like this book. Touch receptors in your skin notice the change—you're touching something new. They instantly send that information along the sensory nerves to your spinal cord. It then travels up to the thalamus (THAL-uh-muhs) part of your brain, which passes it along to the somatosensory

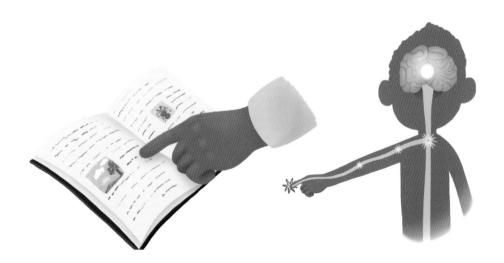

cortex. That's a really big word that just means the part of your brain that says, *Hey! You're touching something. Let me tell you what it is.* And it lets the rest of your brain and body know that you are touching a book.

With the sense of touch, you can also feel temperatures, pressure, a tickle, an itch, vibration, and pain. Your fingertips and lips are the most sensitive to touch because they're packed with touch receptors. Other parts of your body, like your elbow, don't have nearly as many touch receptors, so they're less sensitive. God gave us our sense of touch, and it gives us a ton of information about the world around us.

Close your eyes for just a moment and think about what you feel. Go ahead; I'll do it too. What did you feel? The smooth pages of this book? A pillow or a chair? Did you feel how warm or how cold it is? Now reach up and touch your nose and your hair. God gave you the ability to *feel* what you touch. How awesome and amazing and wonderful is that?

Lord, as I go through the day and touch blankets, trees, and door-knobs, remind me to thank You for this gift of touch. Amen.

EXPLORE THE WONDER

Our skin is always touching something. So why don't we feel our clothes or the air or the chair we're sitting in every moment? The answer is we actually *do* feel them. But our brain is able to ignore those messages. That way, we're not always thinking, *Hey, I'm wearing socks.* And *Hey, I'm still wearing socks.* And *Hey, what do you know? I'm still wearing socks!*

80

FLYING SNAKES?!

We are fighting against the spiritual
powers of evil in the heavenly world.

EPHESIANS 6:12 ICB

Just when you thought this world couldn't get any weirder, you hear about flying snakes. Sounds like something out of a nightmare, right? But in the jungles of South and Southeast Asia, flying snakes are a real thing—except they don't actually fly. It's more like falling with style.

Flying snakes look like any other snake. They don't have actual wings. (How crazy would that be!) And instead of flying, they glide. To take off, a

snake slithers to the end of a branch and launches itself into the air, twisting its body and turning its head to change directions. Because they don't have wings, these snakes can't fly up, only down and sideways. Flying snakes rarely touch the ground. They prefer to stay high in the treetops, gliding from tree to tree to hunt their prey.

Snakes have a pretty rotten reputation. It probably started with that whole mess-up in the garden of Eden when Satan appeared to Adam and Eve looking like a snake. While snakes themselves aren't evil, there is evil in this world. And the devil makes sure it's always flying around, looking for somewhere to land. When someone chooses to be mean, to be selfish, or to talk badly about others, that evil has found a place to land. Make sure it doesn't land in your life by sticking close to God and following Him. That old snake, the devil, doesn't stand a chance against Him!

God, teach me to fill my life with Your goodness and Your Word so evil can't find any place to land. Amen.

Flying lemur

What animal isn't a lemur and can't fly? The flying lemur! Because it can't fly and isn't a lemur, scientists call it by its other name: colugo (kuh-LOO-go). Instead of wings, it has a large flap of skin called a membrane (MEM-breyn) that reaches from its face to its hands, feet, and tail. Using that flap like a hang glider, the colugo soars from tree to tree through its forest home in Southeast Asia—gliding as far as 450 feet!

165

81

A RIVER OF RAINBOWS

Always be joyful. Never stop praying.
Be thankful in all circumstances.

1 THESSALONIANS 5:16-18 NLT

The Caño Cristales River flows with the colors of the rainbow. What makes this river in Colombia, South America, so colorful? It's a tiny underwater plant called *Macarenia clavigera*. From June to December, its flowers bloom in every shade of red, from the palest pink to the darkest red. Add to that yellow sands, green algae, and blue waters, and you have a liquid rainbow about 60 miles long.

The *Macarenia clavigera* is a picky little plant, though. Everything has to be just right for it to bloom. The water can't be too shallow, or it'll dry out. But it can't be too deep, or the plant will die. If it doesn't get enough sunlight, the blooms will be dull. Oh, and it tears easily, so no touching!

Macarenia might be picky about when it blooms, but we shouldn't be. Sometimes we say we're waiting for just the right time to speak up for God. Or we're waiting to finish soccer season or for summer to start before we serve Him. But really, I think we're waiting because we're afraid we'll fail—that the car wash won't raise enough money, our friend won't come to church, or we'll be rejected. Here's the thing: Our job isn't to make sure everything works out. Our job is to serve, to help, and to share God's good news every chance we get. God will take care of the rest. So go ahead: be bold and "bloom" for God whenever and wherever you can.

Lord, I have so many reasons to be joyful, but You are the greatest one! Amen.

EXPLORE THE WONDER

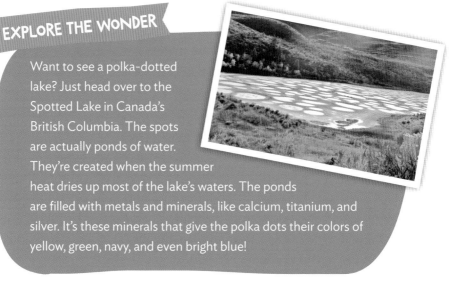

Want to see a polka-dotted lake? Just head over to the Spotted Lake in Canada's British Columbia. The spots are actually ponds of water. They're created when the summer heat dries up most of the lake's waters. The ponds are filled with metals and minerals, like calcium, titanium, and silver. It's these minerals that give the polka dots their colors of yellow, green, navy, and even bright blue!

82

WAITING FOR A SHOOTING STAR

Be devoted to one another in love.

ROMANS 12:10 NIV

Have you ever seen a shooting star? It's a quick streak of light that zips across the nighttime sky. The thing is, that shooting star isn't a star at all. It's a falling meteoroid (MEE-tee-uh-roid), or space rock. Some are as tiny as a piece of dust. Others are up to 330 feet in size—or just a little smaller than a football field. (Larger objects are called asteroids.)

When a meteoroid crashes into Earth's atmosphere, it starts to burn up. That's what causes the bright streak of light, and that's when the meteoroid's name changes to *meteor*, or shooting star. Any chunks that survive that burning trip through the atmosphere and land on Earth have their name changed yet again. They're called *meteorites*.

About 50 tons of space rock hit the Earth's atmosphere every day. Why don't we see them? Well, most are quite small. Others fall into the oceans. Still others fall during the day, when we can't see their light.

Shooting stars are beautiful, but they don't last. Some friendships can be like that too. When a friend has a bad day, makes a mistake, disagrees with you, or needs more of your time, it's easy to let that friendship "burn up" like a meteor passing through the atmosphere. Don't be the kind of friend who "shoots" through someone's life and disappears when it gets tough. Be a true friend. Someone who's there in good times, bad times, and all the times in between. After all, Jesus is that kind of friend to you.

Hoba meteorite in Namibia

The largest meteorite ever found in the US is the Willamette meteorite. Found in 1902, it's made of iron and weighs over 15 tons. But it looks like a pebble compared to the Hoba meteorite found in Namibia. It's about nine feet long, nine feet wide, and three feet thick and weighs over 66 tons—that's about the same as 10 big African elephants!

Lord, You always listen, always help, and always care. Help me be a friend like You. Amen.

83

KNOCKED THE WIND OUT

When he saw the crowds, he
had compassion on them.

MATTHEW 9:36 NIV

You're dribbling the soccer ball down the field while your friend **tries to steal it.** You dodge, you spin, then *bam*! Your friend's elbow hits you right in the stomach. Suddenly, you can't breathe. *At all.* What's going on?

You've had the wind knocked out of you. It can happen if you get socked in the stomach or if you fall and land really hard on your back. The problem is with your diaphragm (DY-uh-fram). That's the big muscle right under your

lungs that helps you breathe. A punch or hard landing can make it spasm (SPAZ-um), or clinch up. Kind of like your hand making a fist. And when that happens, you can't breathe for a moment. Don't panic—it's not serious, even though it feels that way. Curl your knees up to your chest and take slow, deep breaths.

Sometimes seeing others who are hurting can knock the wind out of us too. That's called compassion (kum-PASH-uhn). Jesus felt it when He saw the crowds of people who didn't know God. But He didn't just hurt for them and then walk away. He healed them and helped them! And then He sent His disciples out to teach others about Him. Those disciples now include you and me (Matthew 28:19).

What knocks the wind out of you? Is it foster kids, animals in shelters, or God's Earth being treated like one big garbage dump? Whatever it is, Jesus is sending you to do something about it too.

God, give me compassion for others and send me to share Your light and love in our world. Amen.

EXPLORE THE WONDER

Experts say that deep breathing through your diaphragm helps you relax, slows down your heartbeats, and gets rid of stress. It also clears toxins out of your lungs and gets more oxygen to your body. To practice, breathe in through your nose so that both your belly and your chest expand. Fill your lungs all the way up with air. Slowly breathe out through your mouth. Then, just keep breathing!

84

IS THAT A . . . WALKING PINECONE?

God is my strength.

PSALM 73:26 ICB

Is that a walking pinecone? No! It's an artichoke with a tail. Wait, no, it's a *pangolin*! Pangolins live in Asia and Africa, and they might be one of the most unusual-looking creatures you'll ever see. The pangolin is covered in scales, so you might think it's a reptile. But it's a mammal—the only mammal with scales.

Those scales are made of super-tough keratin (KER-uh-tin). That's the

same stuff as your fingernails. The scales cover its entire body, except for its belly, nose, eyes, and ears. When the pangolin feels vulnerable, or threatened, it rolls up into a tight little ball. Its tough scales form an armor that's practically impossible for enemies to break through. Even lions will give up and walk away!

Vulnerable is a big word, and it's a big feeling. It's how we feel when we're threatened or afraid we'll be hurt. Maybe we're scared of being laughed at or even pushed around. Or we don't want to face a mistake we've made. We just want to curl up in a ball and hide. That works great for the pangolin, but it's not a good plan for us. We need to reach out—to God, to family, and to friends. We weren't made to deal with our worries and fears all by ourselves. Friends can comfort us, grown-ups can help us, and God is always there to fill us with His strength. If you're feeling vulnerable, don't curl up and hide like a pangolin. Reach out instead.

God, when I want to just curl up and hide, please help me to be brave and reach out for help instead. Amen.

EXPLORE THE WONDER

Pangolins really chow down on ants and termites—as many as 200,000 a day! After sniffing out a nest, the pangolin claws it open. To protect itself from angry insects, it closes not only its eyes but also its ears and nose. Then it sticks its super-long and sticky tongue inside the nest to lick up the bugs. That tongue can reach 16 inches long—perfect for slurping insects with every lick!

A SHOT IN THE ARM

He comforts us every time we have
trouble, so that we can comfort
others when they have trouble.

2 CORINTHIANS 1:4 ICB

Let's talk shots—and I don't mean the basketball kind. We're talking about the shots some people choose to get at the doctor's office (along with a lollipop, hopefully). They're called vaccines (vak-SEENS). Doctors use them to help keep people from getting sick from some diseases.

Most vaccines contain a really weak or tiny bit of the virus or bacteria that causes a disease. When someone gets a shot of the vaccine, their body's army

174

of white blood cells springs into action—just like it does when you get sick from an actual virus—and memory cells are created (check out page 24). Then if the real, live germ or virus comes along, those memory cells remember exactly how to fight it off.

Of course, we'd rather skip that whole germ thing completely, right? In fact, we'd rather skip all our problems. But we can use the hard stuff that happens to us to help our friends fight off the not-so-great stuff that happens to them. Like when we weren't invited to *that* cool party everyone else was invited to and learn that it really wasn't the end of the world. Then we can help a friend who's feeling left out when they weren't invited to know that they're still special and important. Just like a vaccine can be one of many things that help people fight off bad diseases, we can help others fight off their problems! And if you end the fight with a lollipop, even better!

God, when I have a problem, help me lean in and learn from it so I can help others when they struggle with a similar problem. Amen.

Penicillium mold

Antibiotics (an-ti-bayh-OT-iks) are medicines that fight germs too. They don't work on viruses, like the cold or flu. But they do kill bacteria. Antibiotics can be given as a shot, a pill, a cream, a spray, eye or ear drops, or a pink, bubblegum-flavored liquid to drink. The first antibiotic was penicillin (pen-uh-SIL-in). It was discovered in 1928 by Alexander Fleming. Want to know what it's made of? Penicillium, also known as mold! *Eww!*

175

86

SPACE JUNK

"If you have two shirts, share with the
person who does not have one."

LUKE 3:11 ICB

Space junk—it could be anything from pieces of old satellites
to a glove dropped by an astronaut. Right now, scientists believe
there are over 100 million pieces of space junk orbiting around the Earth. Over
34,000 of them are at least four inches long. Maybe that sounds too tiny to
worry about. But in space, these pieces are zooming around at over 17,000

miles per hour. At that speed, even a tiny piece can rip through spacesuits, damage satellites, or crash into a spacecraft.

Scientists are working on ways to clean up all the junk. One way is to use a robot spacecraft called *OSCaR* (Obsolete Spacecraft Capture and Removal). *OSCaR* would shoot out nets to capture dead satellites and other debris. Because it's only about the size of a shoebox, scientists imagine sending a whole fleet of *OSCaRs* into space to clean up all the junk.

Do you have any junk taking up space in your life? Probably not leftover pieces of satellites, but maybe it's clothes that don't fit anymore, books you've already read, or toys you've outgrown. Or maybe you have lots of coats, too many shirts, or an extra pair of shoes. What can you do to get rid of the stuff? Go through your room and figure out what you can donate, share with someone else, or recycle. (Be sure to ask your parents first!) You might not need those things, but they can be a huge blessing to someone else. Ask God to guide you to someone you can help.

In February 2018, Elon Musk and his company, SpaceX, launched a cherry red convertible Tesla Roadster into space. It was carried on the Falcon Heavy rocket. Strapped into the driver's seat is a mannequin named Starman. He completed one lap around the Sun in 557 days. NASA officially declared Starman's convertible a celestial object—not junk.

God, You have blessed me with so many things. Help me share what I have with those in need. Amen.

STAND OUT IN THE CROWD

"I chose you to come out of the world."

JOHN 15:19 NLT

When someone says *tiger,* you probably imagine the Bengal tiger with its orange and white fur with black stripes. But some tigers are missing the orange color. They're called white tigers, and they are *very* rare. Hundreds of years ago, white tigers roamed the forests of India. But they were so prized by hunters and collectors that they disappeared from the wild in 1958.

White tigers actually *are* Bengal tigers, but they have a little quirk in their genes. Genes are like God's building instructions for all living things. They determine things like how tall you'll be and the color of your hair. That quirk in the white tiger's genes changes their orange fur to white, and their eyes from yellow to blue. It's called leucism (LOO-si-zem), and it's what makes white tigers really stand out in the tiger crowd.

The things that make us different are often the things that make us stand out. Sometimes, though, blending in seems a lot easier. Maybe you're afraid that being different will get you laughed at or left out. But you know what? Being who God created you to be is *way* better than blending in! If you're a whiz at math, dive into that long division. Think pickleball is better than basketball? Grab a paddle and go. Want to pray before lunch? Ask a friend to join in. God didn't make you to blend in. He made you to stand out.

God, You made me wonderfully different from everyone else. Please give me the courage to stand out in the crowd and be who You created me to be. Amen.

EXPLORE THE WONDER

If you visit Calcasieu Lake in Louisiana, you just might spot Pinky. She's a rare albino dolphin who is completely . . . *pink*! Albino animals have a quirk in their genes that causes them to be born without *any* color in their skin, hair, or eyes. So why is Pinky pink? The blubber under her skin is a reddish color. When it shows through her white skin, she looks bubblegum pink!

THE SKELETON COAST

"I came to give life—life in all its fullness."

JOHN 10:10 ICB

What did the ocean say to the pirate? *Nothing. It just waved!* That may be funny, but the waves around Namibia's Skeleton Coast in Africa are not. The stormy winds there never stop blowing. They whip up the waves and twist the ocean's currents. And the fogs get so thick that captains can't tell where the water ends and the rocky coast begins! All that adds up to a lot of shipwrecks.

The Skeleton Coast is the world's largest ship cemetery, with the "bones" of thousands of ships sticking out of the sand. There are ocean liners, fishing trawlers, gunboats, sailing clippers, and even an old pirate's galleon. It's impossible to count them all, though. The wind keeps moving the sand dunes—covering up some wrecks and uncovering more!

But there's more to this coast than skeletons. Animals like black rhinos, elephants, lions, cheetahs, hyenas, jackals, giraffes, oryx, kudus, zebras, and seals all live there. In fact, it's one of the few places on Earth where all these animals are found together.

God creates rich and diverse life, even in the most unexpected places. That's easy to forget when you're in one of those "unexpected" places. Maybe your neighborhood, school, or church is filled with people from lots of different cultures, and you're not sure where you fit in. That's when you have to choose: stay stuck in the sand, or reach out. Talk to the people around you. Learn where they are from and their favorite foods and traditions. Share some of yours. You can learn so much about the world, yourself, and God when you reach out to people who are different from you—people who are all made in the beautiful image of God.

How does an elephant cross the desert sand? With style! The elephants living along Namibia's Skeleton Coast have adapted to their desert life. That includes learning how to travel over huge dunes of sand—they surf! After climbing to the top of a dune, they use their front legs to pull themselves down, while their back legs simply slide along.

Lord, open my eyes to see the richness and the wonder You have placed in all the different people around me. Amen.

SUIT UP!

Don't worry about anything, but
pray about everything.

PHILIPPIANS 4:6 CEV

Spacesuits aren't just cool-looking costumes. Each suit is like a little person-shaped spacecraft, because these are the suits astronauts wear when they work *outside* the spacecraft. They've got to stand up to all the harshness of outer space, so every detail is important.

To suit up, astronauts first put on a special stretchy bodysuit. Water runs through tubes in the suit to keep astronauts cool. Next comes the upper part of the suit. It's shaped like a sleeveless shirt and is super-strong but light. It connects to all the life support equipment. The sleeves go on separately, then the gloves—which have heaters inside to keep fingers warm. Pants go on next and then the boots. All the "cloth" parts are made of layers that are water-resistant, fire-resistant, and even bulletproof—to protect astronauts from space junk, not bullets! (Read about space junk on page 176.) The suits are white to reflect the heat from the Sun. Suits also have oxygen for breathing, water for drinking, and earphones and microphones for talking to fellow spacewalkers. The whole suit is topped off with a helmet, which even has a small foam block inside for scratching itchy noses!

Just as astronauts need to suit up before stepping out into space, you need to suit up before stepping out into the world. Not with a spacesuit, but with prayer. Ask God to cover your heart, head, hands, and feet with His protection. Ask Him to guide and shield you from all the "junk" in the world. And finally, ask Him to help you reflect the warmth of His love to everyone you meet. Don't forget to suit up!

God, astronauts have suits to help shield them, but I have something even better: You! Remind me to "suit up" every day. Amen.

EXPLORE THE WONDER

Remember Elon Musk's Starman? (If not, check out page 177.) He isn't just wearing jeans and a T-shirt for his spin around the Sun. He's wearing a state-of-the-art SpaceX crew flight suit. It's not just for show, either. Starman is testing the suit out for future missions. With its crisp black and white design, Starman is riding in style.

JUNO AND JUPITER

LORD, there is no one like you!

JEREMIAH 10:6 NLT

Even if you somehow squished all the other planets in our solar system together into one lump, Jupiter would still be bigger. It would take 1,321.3 Earths to fill up this giant planet. Jupiter doesn't have land or water, though. It's a gigantic ball of swirling gases—mostly hydrogen and helium, like the Sun.

In 2011, NASA launched the *Juno* spacecraft on a mission to take a closer look at Jupiter. It arrived in 2016 and has been circling Jupiter ever since. *Juno*'s cameras—called JunoCam—are able to peek behind Jupiter's thick clouds to see what's going on.

Thanks to *Juno*, scientists are learning things they never knew before. For example, Jupiter's north and south poles are much bluer in color—and stormier—than scientists believed. There is also about 10 times less water than they expected to find. And even though Jupiter is made up of gases, they believe it has a solid core at its center. Scientists are hoping to learn even more as *Juno* continues its mission until 2025.

Even though we're learning more all the time, we'll *never* learn everything about space. And we'll never learn everything about God. He's just too big and amazing to ever fully understand. Just imagine, the God who created Earth, Jupiter, and all of space knows and loves *you*! That leaves only one thing for you to do: praise Him! Drop to your knees or throw your arms in the air. Sing, shout, or dance about it—but praise Him. Because there is no one like our God!

Lord, You are awesome and amazing! I want to spend my whole life learning about You, praising You, and glorifying You. Amen.

The Great Red Spot is a massive storm that's been brewing on Jupiter for hundreds of years! Even though astronomers now believe the storm is shrinking a little, it's still 9,800 miles across—big enough for the whole Earth to fit inside! *Juno* recently discovered the Great Red Spot is over 200 miles deep. The Marianas Trench, the deepest spot in Earth's oceans, is "only" about seven miles deep!

91

SLICE RiGHT THROUGH IT

The word of God is . . . sharper than
the sharpest two-edged sword.

HEBREWS 4:12 NLT

With a face like a chainsaw, the sawfish looks like it swam out of the cheesiest scary movie ever. But this fish is real! The largest kind can grow as long as 25 feet. (That's longer than three jump ropes stretched out end to end!)

That chainsaw-looking snout is called a rostrum (RAH-strum). It has sharp teeth all around its edge. It's filled with thousands of sensors that pick up on tiny electrical charges put out by the fish they love to eat. (Actually, all living creatures put out tiny electrical charges—even you and me!) Sawfish use these sensors to locate their prey. Then, with a quick swish-swish of their saw, they slice up their food. Dinnertime!

Chances are, you don't have a chainsaw on your face, but you do have something to help you do some slicing—not through fish but through the devil's lies. You see, pretty much everything the devil says is a lie (John 8:44). But God gives you a weapon—a sword—to fight those lies (Ephesians 6:17). It's the Bible. When you read its words, it will show you what's really true. It cuts through the lies so they can't hurt you.

For example, imagine the devil tells you a lie like *Everybody cheats on tests.* Or *It's just a little lie. Who would it hurt?* Slice right through those lies with the truth of Exodus 20:15 and Colossians 3:9. (Check them out for yourself.) The devil's lies are no match for the sword of God's truth!

God, when the devil lies to me, show me the truth in Your Word that will help me slice right through it. Amen.

EXPLORE THE WONDER

The sawfish's ability to pick up on their prey's tiny electrical charges is called electroreception, and sharks have that ability too. Tiny sensors all over the shark's face can pick up the tiniest movements—even a heartbeat. Electroreception only works from about three feet away. But it helps the shark make sure that first chomp is right on target!

92

WHO'S SHAPING YOU?

Create in me a pure heart, God.

PSALM 51:10 ICB

If you walk through the White Desert National Park, you might think you're on the Moon instead of in Egypt. Miles and miles of white sand are dotted with massive white-chalk rock formations. At sunrise or sunset, all that white reflects the orange and pink hues of the sky. And on nights with a full Moon, the White Desert looks like something from the snow-covered Arctic.

Located in the Sahara, the White Desert has more sculpted rocks than

any other desert in the world. One looks like a giant rabbit getting ready to hop away. Another is called "Chicken and Mushroom." It looks almost exactly like, well, a giant chicken sitting under an even more giant mushroom.

What created all these interesting shapes? The wind. Little by little, year after year, the wind chipped away the white-chalk rocks. And what's been left behind are some of the most interesting and crazily shaped rocks in the world.

Wind shaped the rocks of the White Desert, but what, or who, is shaping you—the way you think, the words you say, and the things you do? A lot of people chase after "stuff" they wish they had, worrying about how they look, and wondering if they're better than someone else. They're shaped by jeal-ousy, selfishness, and pride. If you let yourself be shaped by those things, you're probably not going to like the way you turn out. Even the good people and good things of this world aren't perfect. Only God is perfect, and only He can perfectly shape you. Read His Word. Talk to Him. And trust Him to make you into the person He created you to be.

Crystal Mountain in Egypt

Crews building a road in the White Desert stumbled across an amazing find: a mountain made almost entirely of crystal! It's now called Crystal Mountain, and it's actually more like a large hill. At least 12 different kinds of crystals make up this mountain. It even has a crystal arch big enough to stand under!

Lord, shape me, change me, and make me into exactly who You want me to be. Amen.

93

DON'T GET HANGRY!

We were made right with God by His grace.

TITUS 3:7 ICB

I t's Saturday morning, and you snap at your sister for no reason, growl at the dog, and then flop on the couch because it's raining and you can't go outside. You're just so angry! Suddenly, your stomach rumbles so loud that the dog barks. That's when you remember that you forgot to eat breakfast. You're not just angry; you're hungry too. You're *hangry*.

Hangry is more than just a bad attitude. There's some real stuff going on in your body. One of those things has to do with energy. When you eat, your

rumble grumble!

body turns the food into simple sugars to use for energy. So when you run low on energy, your brain thinks you're in trouble. It sends out the "fight or flight" chemical called adrenaline (uh-DREN-uh-lin). Being hangry makes it harder to control your emotions, and you get upset about things that don't usually bother you. What's the cure? Eat something!

People sometimes act angry when there's actually something else going on. Maybe they're hungry or tired or worried about something. If a friend snaps at you for no reason, don't snap back. Put yourself in their shoes. (I don't mean snatch their sneakers. That would just make them angrier!) Ask yourself what else might be going on and how you could help. Offer to share a snack and listen. Give them a second chance. That's called grace, and God gives you a whole bunch of it every day. Do the same and give others the same grace God gives you.

God, when others mess up, help me to give them grace—just like You give me grace when I mess up. Amen.

EXPLORE THE WONDER

We humans don't like to go long without food. We can get hangry pretty quickly. But some animals can go weeks or even months without anything to eat. And then there's the olm salamander. This cave-dwelling little fellow can survive more than 10 years without eating any food at all!

I SPY A GIGANTIC EYE

Jesus answered, "I am the way. And I am the truth and
the life. The only way to the Father is through me."

JOHN 14:6 ICB

Deep in the Sahara Desert is a gigantic eye—an eye so big it
can be seen from outer space! It's called . . . the Eye of the Sahara.
Dun-dun-duuunnn!

Okay, it's not really an eye. It's a 25-mile-wide crater that *looks* like an eye.
It was formed long, long ago by a massive volcanic eruption that pushed the
ground up. The ground later collapsed down again and was eroded, or worn
away, by wind and water. The blue rings come from the minerals melted by
that eruption, and the pale center is volcanic rock.

Local people have long known about the Eye. But the rest of the world didn't
learn about it until astronauts aboard the *Gemini IV* photographed it from space

The Eye of the Sahara

in the 1960s. These days, soaring over the Eye in a hot-air balloon is a popular thing to do for both tourists and scientists. And today's astronauts still look for the huge eye—it stands out in the middle of all that sand as a landmark to help them navigate.

Navigate (NAV-ih-gate) means to keep a ship, a plane, or even a person headed in the right direction. That's what Jesus does for us. He shows us the way to go. Because throughout our lives, we have lots of choices to make, and knowing what to choose isn't always easy. Like whether to go the baseball game or to church, hang out with your friends or help your grandmother with her garden like you promised, spend all your allowance on that cool new game or save some of it to give to God. Talk to Jesus. Read about the choices He made, and He'll help you navigate your choices every day.

Lord, there are so many choices to make, and it's so hard to make the right choice without You. Help me choose what You would choose. Amen.

EXPLORE THE WONDER

In the Arabic language, *Sahara* means "desert." So when we say, "Sahara Desert," we're really saying, "Desert Desert." The Sahara is the world's largest hot desert; only the cold deserts of Antarctica and the Arctic are bigger. It stretches out 3,629,360 square miles. That makes it just a little bit smaller than the entire United States! The Sahara's summertime temperatures hover around 100 degrees Fahrenheit, but the highest temperature ever recorded was 124.3 degrees in 2018!

SO SENSITIVE

"Do for other people what you
want them to do for you."

LUKE 6:31 ICB

Have you ever wished you could just shrink up and disappear? Maybe you were embarrassed or had your feelings hurt—or you were afraid you *might* get hurt. There's a plant that knows exactly how you feel. Scientists call it *Mimosa pudica*. (*Pudica* means "bashful.") But most people simply call it the sensitive plant. It grows wild in South and Central America. And whenever it's touched or feels threatened, its leaves quickly fold up and droop!

Why so sensitive? Scientists believe it's a kind of self-defense. With its soft leaves and globe-like pink flowers, the sensitive plant looks quite tasty to animals hungry for a little snack. But the sudden movement of its leaves scares off most would-be munchers.

We can be a little sensitive ourselves sometimes. If you have ever been laughed at, left out, or just plain hurt by someone, you know it's no fun. So, like the sensitive plant, we sometimes shrink away from new people and friendships because we don't want to risk getting hurt again. Here's the thing, though: when we aren't willing to risk a little, we miss out on all the good that could come from those new friendships. The best thing to do is to stop thinking about ourselves and think about the other person instead. Because chances are, they're a little afraid of taking a risk too. Ask yourself how you'd want them to reach out to you—and then do the same. Sure, it's a little risky, but it's also full of wonderful possibilities!

God, help me not to shrink away from others but to reach out to them with friendship instead. Amen.

EXPLORE THE WONDER

Sunshine makes the telegraph plant happy. So happy that it just has to dance when the light hits its leaves. It dances to get closer to the light. But this leafy green dancing machine also loves to groove to some music, which is why it's nicknamed the "dancing plant." Scientists aren't completely sure why music makes it move—perhaps some of us are just made to dance!

96

TO THE MOON!

You should be strong. Don't give up, because
you will get a reward for your good work.

2 CHRONICLES 15:7 ICB

Apollo 11 landed on the Moon on July 20, 1969, and Neil Armstrong became the first man to step onto the Moon. He made it look easy. But getting to the Moon wasn't easy at all.

In 1961, President John F. Kennedy announced a goal to land a man on the Moon before the decade ended. So NASA scientists got busy. They first tried to land a probe called *Ranger 3* on the Moon. But it sailed right past the Moon. *Ranger 4*'s instruments didn't work. *Ranger 5* and *Ranger 6* lost power. At last, *Ranger 7* was a success! But that was just the first step. Next, NASA had to figure out how to get a man into space and back to Earth again. Then how to land a spacecraft on the Moon and take off again. For every step there were plenty of failures. NASA scientists had to persevere (pur-suh-VEER). That means they never gave up. They kept learning from every failure until, at last, Armstrong left his footprint on the Moon. And when he did, all the NASA staffers at mission control—along with the rest of the world—cheered!

You may have already figured this out, but you're going to fail sometimes. Fail the test, fail in the game, fail at being a good friend, even fail at following God. But those kinds of failures are only really failures if you give up. *Persevere.* Learn from your mistakes. Apologize. Make some changes. Try again. But never give up, especially on following God. After all, He never gives up on you!

Lord, when things get hard or just don't work out, help me learn from my mistakes and keep moving forward. Amen.

Spacecrafts have come a long way since those early years at NASA. A company called Relativity Space is planning to launch its first rocket in 2021. They're calling it *Terran 1*, and its mission will be to deliver satellites to orbit in space. But what makes *Terran 1* especially cool is that the entire rocket was printed out on special 3-D printers that print with metal!

97

CATCH SOME ZZZZS

You won't need to be afraid when you lie down.
When you lie down, your sleep will be peaceful.

PROVERBS 3:24 ICB

When I was a kid, I loved baseball and hanging out with my friends. Want to know what I didn't love? Naps. I mean, who wants to stop all the fun to rest? But in some countries, people love their naps. In Spain, it's called a *siesta* (see-ES-tuh). And in Japan, it's called an *inemuri* (i-ne-MUH-ri). Some Japanese companies even have napping rooms filled with couches and beds. A few American companies are starting to encourage naps too.

Why all the fuss about naps? Well, NASA did a study to find out. They discovered that when astronauts took a short nap, they were happier, more creative, and more alert when they woke up. But there's a right way to nap. Scientists say the best naps are power naps that last only about 20 to 30 minutes. If you sleep longer, it can be hard to wake up.

There's a story in the Bible about a time Jesus took a nap. He and the disciples were in a boat out on the Sea of Galilee. A terrible storm came up, and the disciples were terrified. But Jesus wasn't worried. In fact, He had grabbed a pillow and was fast asleep. How could Jesus sleep through such a storm? Because He knew His Father was in control and watching over them (Mark 4:35–41). So whether it's stormy in your world or smooth sailing, you can rest knowing that God is watching over you too.

So maybe naps aren't such a terrible thing. In fact, I just might take a little siesta right now . . . zzzz.

Lord, thank You for always watching over me so I can rest without feeling afraid. Amen.

EXPLORE THE WONDER

Napping pods are popping up in libraries, colleges, and hospitals all over the place. It's not an invasion—it's a new way to nap! These pods are built kind of like a bubble and are the perfect size for one person to nap in. Simply climb in, stretch out, and pull down the cover. Gentle music puts you to sleep, and soft lights and a little shake wakes you up again.

98

IF YOU'RE HAPPY AND YOU KNOW IT

This is the day that the Lord has made.
Let us rejoice and be glad today!

PSALM 118:24 ICB

How do you show you're happy? If you're a cat, you purr. If you're a dog, you wag your tail. And if you're a rabbit, you bust out your best binky moves. You read that right—*binky*. When rabbits are happy, they do this crazy kind of move called a binky. Each bunny has its own binky style, but it's a kind of jumping, midair twist with a kick and a little hop or two on the landing. Some bunnies' binkies can reach almost three feet in the air! If you watch a bunny binky, you can't help but be happy too.

So back to that first question: How do *you* show your happiness? Sure, there are tough days, but there are also wonderful days when everything seems to go your way. You wake up to your favorite breakfast, ace the test, and find an extra dollar in your pocket. There are days when God blesses you with a chance to help a friend or the opportunity to learn something new about Him. And there are so-so days that are still amazing because You get to share them with Him. So how do you let the world know life is good? Smile, sing, whistle, or dance—whatever says "happy" to you. Just be sure to thank the One who gave you all those reasons to be happy. Praise Him, say a prayer of thanks, and tell someone how good God is to you. And hey, if you feel like it, bust out a binky or two—that's what the bunnies do!

Lord, thank You for all the wonders, the fun, and the happiness You pour into my days. Amen.

SHARE THE WONDER

Share your happiness by helping someone else feel happy too. Use the word *JOY* to remind you to do these three things every day: (1) do something to make Jesus happy, (2) do something to make others happy, and (3) do something to make yourself happy too. Here's a secret: when you help others, you not only make them happy, but you make Jesus and yourself happy too!

99

NO IFS ABOUT IT

Whoever believes in the Son has eternal life.

JOHN 3:36 NIV

Firenadoes, derecho winds . . . what else does nature have up its sleeve? Ice volcanoes, of course! But don't worry, these aren't dangerous. They're just cool. Actually, they're cold. Really, *really* cold!

Ice volcanoes can form along the shores of large lakes, like Lake Michigan, if the conditions are just right. Temperatures must stay below freezing (32 degrees Fahrenheit) for days and days at a time. The freezing temperatures will create a thin layer of ice near the shore. If the wind blows in powerful enough waves, sprays of water can burst up through that layer of ice in places. Then, if the air is cold enough, the water drops will freeze around the hole they spurted up through. Over time, the freezing water creates a cone-like mound that looks a lot like a miniature volcano made of ice.

If the temperatures are just right, *if* the wind is powerful, *if* the waves are strong, then you might get an ice volcano. That's a lot of ifs. Some people think that getting to heaven has a lot of ifs. *If* you obey all the rules, *if* you never mess up, *if* you work really, really hard, then you might get to heaven. But God doesn't do ifs. He does promises. Believe that Jesus is His Son (John 3:36), love and follow Him (John 12:26), and He'll take you home with Him to heaven (John 14:3). There are no ifs about it.

Lord, thank You for being a God of promises. I know I can trust You to keep every single one! Amen.

202

A 45-foot-tall ice volcano has formed in the country of Kazakhstan. Unlike most ice volcanoes that form over cold water, this one forms over a hot spring. Sprays of spring water erupt out of the hollow cone, freeze, and fall back onto the ice, gradually making its tower grow taller and taller!

THE GREAT CONJUNCTION

Since the world began, no ear has heard
and no eye has seen a God like you, who
works for those who wait for him!

ISAIAH 64:4 NLT

Imagine that Jupiter and Saturn are running a race around the Sun. But Jupiter is a much faster runner than Saturn. It takes Jupiter about 12 Earth years to circle, or orbit, around the Sun, while it takes Saturn about

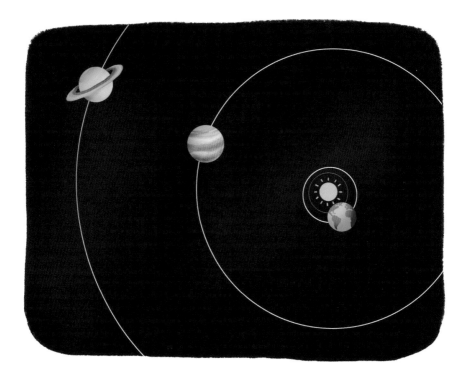

30 years. So every 20 years Jupiter catches up. For one night, they appear to be side-by-side. If you're looking up at them from Earth, that is. In reality, they're still 456 million miles apart.

When two celestial bodies—like the planets, moons, and stars in the sky—come together like that, it's called a conjunction (kun-JUNK-shun). When the two biggest bodies in our solar system, Jupiter and Saturn, come together, it's called a Great Conjunction.

Just as Saturn and Jupiter are always spinning through their orbits, God is always working in the universe, in the world, and in your life. There is not one second in all of eternity when God is not present. Sometimes His work is invisible to you, but every once in a while, God will suddenly burst into the story of your life in a powerful, miracle-working way—a Great Conjunction! It might be in the way He answers a prayer or in the way He makes the impossible possible. Or it might be in a big, bold, and indescribably wonderful way that you could have never imagined. One thing is certain, though: He is always there and always working. So keep your eyes open and be on the lookout for your next Great Conjunction with God!

Lord God, only You are God—and I cannot wait to see what You do with the wonderful story of my life! Amen.

INDEX

LOUiE GiGLiO is the pastor of Passion City Church and the original visionary of the Passion movement, which exists to call a generation to leverage their lives for the fame of Jesus. Since 1997, Passion has gathered collegiate-aged young people in events across the US and around the world, and it continues to see 18–25-year-olds fill venues across the nation. Most recently, Passion hosted over 700,000 people from over 150 countries online at Passion 2021. In addition to the Passion Conferences, Louie and his wife, Shelley, lead the teams at Passion City Church, sixstepsrecords, Passion Publishing, and the Passion Global Institute. Louie is the national bestselling author of *Don't Give the Enemy a Seat at Your Table*, *Not Forsaken*, *Goliath Must Fall*, *Indescribable*, *How Great Is Our God*, and *The Comeback*. Louie and Shelley make their home in Atlanta, Georgia, with their goldendoodle, London.

NiCOLA ANDERSON has been an illustrator and graphic designer since she could hold a crayon in her hand but has been working professionally since 2001. After many years working in the design industry, she now crafts imaginary worlds from her home studio, AndoTwin Studio, in Manchester, UK. During this time, she has worked with an eclectic range of clients and has loved every minute!

The Wonder of Creation

© 2021 Louie Giglio

Tommy Nelson, PO Box 141000, Nashville, TN 37214

Published in Nashville, Tennessee, by Tommy Nelson. Tommy Nelson is an imprint of Thomas Nelson. Thomas Nelson is a registered trademark of HarperCollins Christian Publishing, Inc.

The writer is represented by Cyle Young of C.Y.L.E. (Cyle Young Literary Elite, LLC), a literary agency.

Tommy Nelson titles may be purchased in bulk for educational, business, fund-raising, or sales promotional use. For information, please email SpecialMarkets@ThomasNelson.com.

Note: As new scientific research is verified, some data within the book may not reflect the latest findings. As we become aware, we will make editorial updates to this book when appropriate.

ISBN 978-1-4002-3059-4 (audiobook) ISBN 978-1-4002-3058-7 (eBook) ISBN 978-1-4002-3046-4 (HC)

Library of Congress Cataloging-in-Publication Data

Names: Giglio, Louie, author. | Fortner, Tama, 1969- author. | Anderson, Nicola (Illustrator), illustrator.
Title: The wonder of creation : 100 more devotions about god and science / Louie Giglio with Tama Fortner ; illustrated by Nicola Anderson.
Description: Nashville, Tennesse : Thomas Nelson, 2021. | Series: Indescribable kids | Includes index. | Audience: Ages 6-10 | Summary: "The Wonder of Creation, Louie Giglio's third devotional for kids following the wildly popular Indescribable and How Great Is Our God, explores the magnificence of creation with fascinating STEM facts, vibrant illustrations, and a wonder-filled celebration of God's glorious world"-- Provided by publisher.
Identifiers: LCCN 2021019614 (print) | LCCN 2021019615 (ebook) | ISBN 9781400230464 (hardcover) | ISBN 9781400230587 (epub)
Subjects: LCSH: Religion and science--Prayers and devotions--Juvenile literature. | BISAC: JUVENILE NONFICTION / Religious / Christian / Science & Nature | JUVENILE NONFICTION / Religious / Christian / Devotional & Prayer
Classification: LCC BL243 .G55 2021 (print) | LCC BL243 (ebook) | DDC 261.5/5--dc23
LC record available at https://lccn.loc.gov/2021019614
LC ebook record available at https://lccn.loc.gov/2021019615

Written by Louie Giglio with Tama Fortner
Illustrated by Nicola Anderson

Printed in South Korea

21 22 23 24 25 SAM 6 5 4 3 2 1

Mfr: SAM / Seoul, South Korea / October 2021 / PO #12092163